Buon Gusto!

Buon Gusto!

The Best Recipes from Five Top Italian Restaurants in Toronto

Val Clery

AN ARCADIA HOUSE BOOK

MACMILLAN OF CANADA
A Division of Canada Publishing Corporation
Toronto, Ontario, Canada

BUON GUSTO!
The Best Recipes from Five Top
Italian Restaurants in Toronto
Copyright © 1987 by Arcadia House Inc.

AN ARCADIA HOUSE BOOK
Jack Jensen
Thad McIlroy

Canadian Cataloguing in Publication Data

Clery, Val, date.
  Buon gusto! : the best recipes from five
top Italian restaurants in Toronto

Includes index.
ISBN 0-7715-9474-7

1. Cookery, Italian.   2. Restaurants, lunch rooms,
etc. – Ontario – Toronto.   I. Title.

TX723.C54 1986   641.5945   C86-093973-1

Design and illustrations: David Montle
Photography: Rolf Heinecke
Typeset by Thad McIlroy at McCutcheon Graphics on an Apple
Macintosh Plus™ using Ready,Set,Go! 3® and output in Palatino™
on a LaserWriter Plus™

Cover Photograph: Scampi Giulia from San Lorenzo (page 143)

Macmillan of Canada
A Division of Canada Publishing Corporation

Printed and Bound in Canada by
Friesen Printers, Altona, Manitoba

CONTENTS

FOREWORD   7

SHOPPING ITALIAN   11

BINDI RISTORANTE   20

CIBO RISTORANTE   48

ORSO   71

PRONTO RISTORANTE   103

RISTORANTE SAN LORENZO   131

GLOSSARY OF ITALIAN TERMS   155

INDEX   157

FOREWORD

At its roots, Toronto is an Anglo-Celtic city. And even today its heavy downtown mixture of old and new architecture, famously clean and orderly, appears to confirm those beginnings. But anyone at all familiar with the city's ethnic evolution in this century will understand why it is so fitting to offer a book about Italian restaurants in Toronto.

An inquisitive stroll through certain shopping districts in midtown and uptown Toronto would soon impress on any stranger the depth of the Italian presence here. In fact, with over 300,000 citizens of Italian origin, Ontario's capital can justifiably claim the largest Italian community outside Italy.

The accumulation of Italian immigration has been gradual since the turn of the century. Some of the earliest arrivals turned to what they knew best, the land, an inclination still confirmed by outlying rural communities with names such as Bronte and Palermo. Most new arrivals, however, gathered in the city, motivated by the understandable ambition to save enough dollars to head back to their homeland and buy a small farm. And most of those early arrivals were men, single or divided from families, who lived in humble rooming houses and cooked the simplest and cheapest food there for themselves. Italian restaurants were almost unheard of.

Eventually, after the end of World War II, the promises of the New World began to encourage immigrants from Italy to bring families with them and to settle here. Building and industrial development in the expanding city and its metropolitan hinterland became increasingly the prime source of livelihood among Italian immigrants.

The highrises and highways of modern Toronto may be seen as monuments to their energy, skill and ambition.

The home is by tradition the hub of Italian daily life, and so the overriding desire of every new family here was to own a home of its own, a place to raise a family, to share with close relatives and, of course, to prepare the kind of food that Italians particularly appreciate. Specialty stores stocking the ingredients for such cooking multiplied and soon even supermarkets began to make a point of offering what their very particular Italian customers sought.

Because at the time Italian immigrant life did tend to centre on the home, restaurants serving authentic Italian cuisine were slow to appear in the city. To be sure, in the 1960s and early 1970s, there were pizza parlours and spaghetti houses serving what North Americans conceived Italian food to be, just as there were restaurants serving chop suey and fried rice and wonton soup as representative of "true" Chinese cuisine. But neither kind gave more than a hint of the richness and the variety that Italian and Chinese families enjoyed at home.

No food writer has made Mediterranean food more familiar in the English-speaking world than Elizabeth David. But in her book, *Italian Food*, published in 1954, she made the very astute point that, in reality, there is no such thing as Italian food, that even in their homeland Italians mostly think of food in entirely regional terms, as Neapolitan or Roman or Venetian food.

It is worth remembering that, like Canada, Italy only quite recently became a unified country with adequate communications. Only in the extreme north are frontiers shared with other cultures and cuisines. What was cooked and eaten in the various regions of the narrow mountain-spined peninsula depended originally on proximity to the sea or on the climate and the nature of the immediate terrain. This resulted in a range of cuisines that neither Italians nor the rest of us who love good food have reason to regret.

Toronto's appreciation of the wealth of Italian cuisine has increased immensely in the past ten years. Young Canadian-born professionals of Italian origin, and other Canadians who have vacationed in Europe or who have been caught up in what might be called the Gourmet Revolution have created a demand for Italian food that far transcends such North American adoptions as pizza and spaghetti with meatballs.

By coincidence, the essentials of authentic Italian cuisine suit the appetite and lifestyle of the 1980s: the quick and simple cooking of fresh ingredients and the preference for fish and light meats over fatty red meats appeal to a generation that is intensely health and weight conscious. And conveniently, the techniques of Italian cooking also make it possible for restauranteurs to satisfy a generation of customers who greatly value time.

The five Italian restaurants featured in this book are comparatively new. Are they more authentically Italian in their food than their predecessors? Perhaps only in the sense that their chefs, young mostly and only rarely Italian, seem more adventurously open to the entire range of Italian regional cuisine and ready to adapt it to the taste of their customers.

While professional catering demands a great deal of

preparatory organization, individual dishes in the chosen restaurants are usually cooked to order, a fact that greatly simplified the adaptation of recipes for home cooking; each recipe has been reshaped to serve four people. Italians insist on using the correct ingredients even at home, and we found little difficulty in obtaining what we needed in Toronto stores. They should be obtainable in most major North American cities.

It has been fairly argued that Europe owes its culinary origins principally to Italy. It is only fair that Italy should still be in the forefront in offering us one of life's greatest pleasures, the pleasure of eating well.

Buon appetito!

SHOPPING ITALIAN

Because Canadians of Italian origin retain a great love of the authentic cuisine of their original homeland, most cities where Italians have settled have soon encouraged specialty Italian food stores to open, and even supermarkets in Italian neighborhoods have recognized the good sense of offering many of the food staples that Italian customers insist on. Because of the growing attractiveness of cooking in the Italian style, even stores in localities where there is no great Italian presence have begun to stock such useful foods as pasta, canned plum tomatoes, and Italian cheeses and preserved meats.

The long, hard winters in most parts of Canada are, happily enough, balanced by warm, fruitful summers benign enough to allow the cultivation locally of much of the fresh produce on which good Italian cooking so depends. And, given the enterprise of the North American mass marketing industry, even in our bleakest months, fresh produce from the southern United States, Mexico and the Caribbean reaches our specialty stores and supermarkets. Some fresh produce from Europe has begun to arrive as well, but for the most part Europe, and in particular Italy itself, sustains a vast regular trade in more stable products not produced reliably here but needed for Italian cooking.

Canadian public health regulations do prohibit the importation of a few Italian specialties, such as raw milk cheeses and certain preserved meats. But for the most part locally produced substitutes for these have almost equalled the quality of the originals. The bulk of the hard wheat vital to the production of pasta comes from Canada. Pasta purists argue endlessly on whether the best of the pasta now manufactured in Canada is as good as the pasta made in Italy from Canadian grain. But such arguments about food, particularly when pursued at table, are never boring and possibly do help to stimulate appetites.

Here are some of the ingredients you may need for your own ventures in Italian cooking:

Anchovies:
While not much used by any of the chefs who have contributed to this book, a filet or two as seasoning can enhance the flavor of fish dishes and sauces that go with them. Generally available in small cans, packed in vegetable or olive oil. Invariably very salty, so use with care.

Beans:
Both dried and ready-cooked canned versions of the wide variety of beans used by Italian cooks are available in Italian food stores and in some food markets. The canned kind are useful to have in the store cupboard for reinforcing soups and other dishes at short notice. But reconstituting and slow-cooking dried beans offers a sort of comforting therapy for inveterate cooks.

Butter:
Butter is used extensively, with or instead of olive oil, in Northern Italian cooking. Because it tends to distort the process of properly seasoning a dish, salted butter is not recommended for cooking. Those who substitute margarine do so at their own risk.

Cheeses:
Locally made substitutes for Italian hard cheeses such as
Parmesan (Parmeggiano) and Romano (Pecorino) may be
cheaper, but satisfy the palates of few professional cooks.
For dishes intended to be memorable, the expense of the
imported quality is usually worthwhile. All the more popular kinds of Italian soft and semi-soft cheeses are made
here with reasonable success and can be found in Italian
cheese stores and the more enterprising of supermarkets.

Fish:
In response to a recent and healthful public inclination to
eat more fish, merchants in major cities have greatly
improved the supply of fresh and frozen fish. Because of
the proximity of the sea to most parts of Italy, fish has
always played an important role in Italian diet. Unfortu-
nately, these days, with pollution increasing in the Mediterranean, Italians in their homeland are not much better
supplied than most urban Canadians. The immense coast-
lines of Canada and the U.S. provide ready supplies of
most kinds of fish common on Italian menus, a lot of it of
better quality. Fish freezes better than meat, but of course
fish that is fresh or that has been stored chilled on ice is
superior in flavor when cooked. A rich variety of shellfish
is almost always available here and is generally excellent
in quality.

Fresh Vegetables:
All the vegetables mentioned in our recipes are available,
excellent in quality, during the summer in major Canadian cities, either from food or farmers' markets. Most of

them, imported, can be found in the more venturesome stores during the rest of the year. Plum tomatoes, an essential in good Italian cooking, can now be obtained during most of the summer.

Herbs:
The virtue of fresh herbs in cooking is being recognized by an increasing number of home cooks; the market gardeners supplying a range of fresh herbs has not kept pace with the demand, even with the demand from professional caterers. A few enterprising greengrocers do manage to offer the more popular varieties during the summer and most urban farmers' markets have a range of herbs on offer. Some chefs provide for themselves by growing herbs both outdoors and under glass. Home cooks can help themselves by preserving a stockpile of the more frequently used herbs during the summer. Basil, a runaway favorite among Italian cooks, can be gently reduced in either butter or olive oil and frozen in usable quantities. Sprigs of thyme, rosemary, dill and sage can be rinsed, quick-frozen, compressed in foil or plastic wrap and kept frozen for later use. Preserved and thawed herbs will never be quite as vivid in flavor as when they were fresh, but they may have a slight edge in subtlety over dried versions.

Meat:
In its use of fresh meat, Italian cuisine may be economical in quantity but never in quality. The demand for veal here has been met in major cities; even the Provimi veal prized by the discriminating and well-off is available. Canadian

beef and pork need no alibis. And if you seek aggressively, you can find free-range poultry.

Mushrooms:
Again demand has ignited enterprise: the more exotic and flavorsome sorts of fungus are now being cultivated and marketed in British Columbia and elsewhere and are available in the more alert food stores. They play a modest but important part in fine Italian cooking. Porcini (cepes) are more often imported dried; while they may seem expensive in that form, their reconstituted flavor makes them a good buy.

Nuts:
Pine nuts (pignoli) have recently acquired a fashionable eminence. They are elusive but, with diligence, can be found. No substitute will do; used with care, they are worth their weight in gold. Hazelnuts, also popular in Italian cooking, are sometimes hard to find. Almonds and walnuts are always plentiful.

Oil:
Olive oil, of course, oils the wheels of Italian digestion. Its hierarchy of grades from the highest cold-pressed extra virgin down to the bottom-of-the-barrel cooking kind are appraised with the same attentiveness as vintages of wine. The idea of extra virginity, whether coldly or hotly pressed, does not strike Italian oleophiles as at all ludicrous: the subtle graduations of flavor are what count. Extra virgin is best savored, uncooked, in small quantities on antipasti or salads. The lower grades, with

their fuller flavors, are fine for cooking, but are sometimes modulated by combination with butter. For certain delicate foods, such as fish, chefs are inclined to prefer lighter vegetable oils.

Pasta:
Understandably, the qualities of pasta are matters also given profound consideration by Italian gourmets. Freshly made pasta has acquired a certain eclat in sophisticated cooking circles in Canada over the past few years and even supermarkets have begun to stock a form of fresh pasta that keeps well under refrigeration. But pasta purists insist that the cooked texture of this mass-produced fresh pasta is inferior because the dough from which it is made is mechanically extruded rather than being rolled out in the traditional fashion. Some pasta lovers claim that, in its more ornate forms the fried version is superior to fresh when cooked. And as mentioned already, a further debate centres on whether Canadian-made dried pasta is the equal of Italian made. We leave judgement to the palate of the diner.

Preserved Meats:
With the few exceptions mentioned already, the result of public health prohibitions, most kinds of Italian preserved meats are widely available in Canada. Given the fine quality of meat used in manufacture, many such Italian specialties made here are quite as good as those available at home.

Preserved Vegetables:
No spread of antipasti on an Italian table would be complete without a small bowl of olives. Unquestionably the
best olives are those imported from the Mediterranean
region, preferably in bulk so that they can be sampled and
judged at time of purchase. They come from Italy, Greece
and Spain, almost always preserved and matured in
brine, which is sometimes spiked with herbs or pepper; jet
black, rich purple and jade, olive green of course (often
stuffed with scarlet pimento). As any afficiando will tell
you, olives are as diverse in character as people and
should be appreciated as such. Canned California olives
are, alas, as uniform and lifeless as automatons. They
are for people who do not like olives. At one time, not
many years ago, in the late summer and fall the roof tiles
of every rural home in southern Italy used to be covered
with split tomatoes drying in the sun. Sun-dried tomatoes provided a vital ingredient of Italian cuisine
throughout the winter. Although canned tomato concentrate and canned whole tomatoes removed the need to
dry tomatoes, they did not efface completely a liking for
the unique flavor and texture of dried tomatoes. And
lately in North America the special qualities of sun-dried
tomatoes, preserved in olive oil, have won them a special
status among chefs and gourmets. The virtues of canned
tomatoes are unquestionable; with admirable patriotism,
Italian chefs working here tend to favor brands imported
from their homeland, but plum tomatoes grown and
canned here are not noticably inferior.

Rice:
For the making of risotto, imported Arborio rice is second to none. It may be slightly more expensive than other kinds of short-grain rice but it remains irreplaceable.

Vinegar:
Ordinary wine vinegars, red or white, are not greatly superior whether they come from Italian, French, California or Canadian vineyards. But Balsamic vinegars, often well-aged and usually highly-priced, like the grander grades of olive oil, add a flavor to food, and particularly to salads, that puts them in a class of their own.

WHERE TO SHOP:
In Toronto:
The localities in Toronto and its metropolitan rim where Italians live and shop have increased greatly since the turn of the century and this migration has not ceased yet. Fortunately, Torontonians of Italian origin do like to live together, so it is not difficult to isolate the shopping areas where Italian ingredients may be bought. The original Little Italy is on College Street between Bathurst and Dufferin, and there is still a fine range of food stores, cheese stores and butchers to choose from. A few Italian stores remain on Danforth Avenue east of Coxwell. St. Clair Avenue West between Christie and Lansdowne is now the main street of Italian shopping, its clothing stores outrivalling its food stores in luxurious variety. Eglinton Avenue West used to be much more an Italian neighborhood, but there are only a few Italian stores left to the west of Oakwood. Further west, Mississauga is

developing a distinctive Italian community. The same is true of Woodbridge to the north. Two chains of stores, La Grotta del Formaggio, with 7 outlets in the Toronto region, and Il Centro del Formaggio, with 4 outlets, offer a varied selection of excellent Italian staples.

In Ottawa:
The vicinity of Preston Street, dubbed *Corsa Italia* during a recent state visit by Italy's president, offers a number of specialty stores.

In Montreal:
Like Toronto, Montreal has attracted many Italian immigrants. Most of their shopping is done on these streets: rue St-Laurent, rue Jean Talon, rue Dante and rue St-Zotique.

In Vancouver:
Lovers of Italian food head for Commercial Drive and Granville Island to shop. The food section of Woodwards store also carries some Italian foods.

In Winnipeg:
The most reliable retailer of Italian foods is said to be De Luca's Specialty Foods Limited at 950 Portage Avenue.

All the recipes in this book have been provided by the chefs of the Toronto restaurants it deals with. They have been specially adapted for home cooking, each redesigned to yield four servings.

Bindi

Giacomo "Jack" Guenzi

*T*he uptown stretch of Yonge Street where Bindi stands might seem an unusual place for a fashionable Italian restaurant. Only a few years ago opening such a place there was obviously a greater risk than it is today: a Greek restaurant that preceded Bindi at this address failed and went bankrupt.

But when Bindi did open the neighborhood had already begun to undergo a subtle and significant generational change. The homes in surrounding streets were being inherited or bought by fairly affluent young couples, more readily attracted to good and unusual food than were the parents and older homeowners whom they replaced.

While they may protest the slightly mocking title of Yuppies, they are to a high degree young urban professionals, not yet rich perhaps but well enough off to regard dining out a reasonable and affordable form of entertainment. For the many with young families, the proximity of a restaurant as interesting and as estimable as Bindi makes it doubly attractive; babysitters proscribe protracted nights out. In addition, in 1982 when the new restaurant opened, the public appetite for Italian food, and particularly for the light and imaginative cucina nuova, was approaching its zenith.

The majority co-owner and maestro of Bindi Ristorante, Giacomo "Jack" Guenzi, had been seeking a suitable site for a restaurant of his own for many years; judging from the amount of business he now regularly attracts, he did find exactly the right spot. He is a stocky, energetic and likable Northern Italian, too matter-of-fact to have much patience with pretentious terms such as cucina nuova, but offering from his menu the range of colorful, flavorsome but non-fattening dishes his young health-aware clients approve of. Such a cuisine is not a demanding challenge since it coincides quite closely with the regional cuisine of Northwest Italy where he grew up, more akin to the cooking of Southern France than to that of Southern Italy.

It is token to the impact of the owner's experience and personality that the restaurant's cooking so exactly and so engagingly reflects his regional Italian origins, because none of his kitchen team are Italian. But then restaurant kitchens, at the more advanced level, do tend to be very multicultural. Style these days is quite as important as authenticity and, at the moment, this style of Italian cuisine is among the most desirable.

The Bindi style of cooking is very evident after a glance through one of its menus, which are often revised and supplemented. There is a noticeable leaning towards seafood, not only as an entree but also in the antipasti and pasta sections of the menu; also shown is a bias towards chicken, another main ingredient much esteemed as healthful nowadays. And the heavy range of veal entrees encountered on more traditional Italian menus is absent.

The experience of eating at Bindi confirms the lightness and grace implied by its menu. Sauces are rarely thickened by flour but consist of reduced cooking juices, sometimes enriched by fresh cream. Both the texture and the color of vegetables are treated with respect. The same deference is accorded to seafood and meat, which are almost invariably cooked to order. The emphasis on freshness is very evident, and the judicious use of fresh herbs, which Jack Guenzi grows himself, is a hallmark of the cuisine.

The decor of Bindi Ristorante mirrors the simple statements of the menu. It is a long narrow room, varied by a raised section near the entrance, with white stucco walls and chairs of pale wood. The compact open kitchen is at the back and there is a small bar up front to help sedate the appetites of those impatient to find a table.

As befits what functions in part as a neighborhood restaurant, Bindi is a relaxed and informal place. The number of patrons who seem to know Jack and his wife personally is a testament to their success. It is never a quiet place, but then it is a very Italian characteristic to approach what you love with gusto. And what you are presented at the tables here almost always inspires such enthusiasm.

BINDI RISTORANTE, 3241 Yonge Street. Telephone: 487-2881. Lunch served from noon to 2.30 p.m. Monday to Friday; dinner served from 5 to 11 p.m. Monday to Saturday. Closed Sundays and all statutory holidays. Fully licensed. Major cards accepted. Reservations recommended.

ANTIPASTI

INSALATA DI FRUTTI DI MARE
Seafood Salad

---

2 cups (475 mL) fish stock or mixture of clam juice and white wine

8 oz. (225 g) small squid, cleaned and thinly sliced across

4 oz. (115 g) bay scallops, halved

4 oz. (115 g) small octopus, head and bone removed

4 oz. (115 g) baby shrimp, cooked and peeled

1 tea bag

1/2 cup (120 mL) olive oil

1/4 cup (60 mL) lemon juice

1 clove garlic, minced

1 filet anchovy, pulverized

2 tbsp. (30 mL) parsley, coarsely chopped

1 tbsp. (15 mL) fresh rosemary leaves, coarsely chopped

- Put 1-1/2 cups (355 mL) fish stock and the sliced squid in saucepan and bring to a gentle simmer. Cook until squid begins to feel tender, then add scallops. Simmer for a few more minutes until both are tender. Remove from heat, drain seafood and set aside to cool. Refrigerate stock for other use.

- Meanwhile put octopus and remaining stock in saucepan and bring to a gentle simmer. Add tea bag to ensure tenderness and continue to simmer. When octopus turns white under outer brown coating and feels tender, drain and discard cooking liquid and tea bag. Rub brown skin and suckers from surface of octopus under cold running water. Discard small bone in head. Slice crossways as thinly as possible and leave to cool.

- An hour before serving, combine squid, scallops,

1 tsp. (5 mL) pink pep-
  percorns
Salt and freshly
  ground black pepper
1 tsp. (5 mL) capers,
  drained and minced
1/4 head bib lettuce
1 tomato, cut in
  wedges
1/2 lemon, thinly sliced

octopus and shrimp.
Thoroughly mix oil, lemon
juice, garlic, herbs, anchovy,
peppercorns and capers,
seasoning to taste with salt
and pepper. Toss dressing
through seafood and chill
until time to serve.

- Spoon salad onto a bed of
  lettuce, garnish with tomato
  wedges and lemon slices.

COZZE ALLA MARINARA
Steamed Mussels with Tomato Sauce

3-4 lbs. (1.35-1.80 kg)
  fresh cultured mus-
  sels
2/3 cup fresh (155 mL)
  marinara sauce (see
  page 36)
1 tbsp. (15 mL) garlic,
  minced
1 tbsp. (15 mL) shallot,
  minced
1 tbsp. (15 mL) sweet
  butter
Parsley sprigs

- Scrub and beard mussels,
  discarding any that are open.
- Put remaining ingredients,
  apart from butter and
  parsley, in shallow heavy
  saucepan and bring to boil.
  Cover, reduce heat slightly
  and cook for 3-4 minutes,
  when all mussels should
  have opened. Discard any
  that have not.
- Divide mussels, still in
  shells, into four warm soup
  bowls. Stir and melt butter
  into sauce and spoon over
  mussels. Garnish with
  parsley before serving.

ANTIPASTO CALDO SAN GIACOMO
Warm Seafood Salad

1/2 lb. (225 g) bay
  scallops
1/2 lb (225 g) monkfish
  (lotte), cut into small
  cubes
1-1/2 cups (355 mL) fish
  stock
3 young carrots,
  julienned
3/4 cup (175 mL) San
  Giacomo dressing
  (see below)
1/4 head bib lettuce

- Put scallops, monkfish and stock in saucepan and bring gently to boil. Add carrots, again bring to boil, then remove and drain carrots and allow seafood to simmer until cooked but still firm.
- Drain seafood and mix it, still warm, with dressing in a bowl. Cool and refrigerate stock for other use.
- Divide warm salad onto bed of torn lettuce on four plates, garnished with julienned carrot. Serve at once.

SAN GIACOMO DRESSING
(For Antipasto)

1/2 cup (120 mL) olive
  oil
2 tbsp. (30 mL) coarsely
  crushed mustard seed
3 tbsp. (45 mL) lemon
  juice
Salt

- Mix oil, mustard seed and lemon juice, seasoning to taste. Keep at room temperature until warm salad is ready.

ZUPPE

ZUPPA D'AMARENA FREDDA
Cold Cherry Soup with Pernod

19 oz. (560 mL) can of
   pitted cherries with
   juice
2 cups (475 mL) cold
   water
1-1/2 tsp. (7 mL) sugar
1-1/4 oz. (35 mL) Pernod
2 tbsp. (30 mL) lemon
   juice
2 pinches cinnamon
1 tsp. (5 mL) cornstarch
1/4 cup (60 mL) table
   cream

- Process all ingredients
  except cornstarch and cream
  in blender or food processor
  until completely liquid. Bring
  to boil, remove from heat
  and blend in cornstarch.
  Return to boil, stirring, then
  chill thoroughly.
- Serve in chilled bowls,
  garnished with a swirl of
  cream.

ZUPPA POMODORA AL FINNOCCHIO
Tomato and Fennel Soup

1 onion, finely chopped
1 clove garlic, minced
1 tbsp. (15 mL) sweet
   butter
1 cup (235 mL) chicken
   stock
2 cups (475 mL) canned
   plum tomatoes,
   drained and chopped

- In saucepan, sauté onion
  and garlic in butter until
  soft. Add chicken stock,
  tomatoes, paste, wine and
  lemon juice. Bring to boil
  and simmer for 15 minutes.
  Stir well, add fennel and
  simmer for 3 minutes more.
- Stir in beurre manié, broken

2 tbsp. (30 mL) tomato
paste
1/2 cup (120 mL) dry
white wine
2 tbsp. (30 mL) fresh
lemon juice
1 bulb fresh fennel,
with leaves, chopped
Salt and freshly
ground black pepper
2 pinches nutmeg
4 tbsp. (60 mL) beurre
manié (see page 36)
1/4 cup (60 mL)
whipping cream

into small pieces, a little at
time. When soup begins to
thicken, remove from heat.
Season to taste with salt
and pepper, add nutmeg and
stir again.
■ Serve in warm bowls,
garnishing each serving
with a spoonful of whipped
cream.

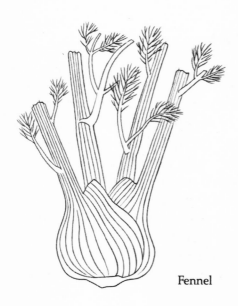

Fennel

INSALATE

INSALATA DELLA CASA
House Salad

2/3 head Romaine lettuce, torn up, washed and shaken dry
2/3 head Boston lettuce, torn up, washed and shaken dry
1/2 cup (120 mL) Bindi house dressing (see page 31)
2 tbsp. (30 mL) pine-nuts, toasted
1 small young carrot, finely julienned

- Mix both kinds of lettuce well together, pour on dressing and toss thoroughly.
- Divide into four servings in bowls, sprinkle each with nuts and garnish with juliennes of carrot.

SALSA PER INSALATA
Oil and Vinegar Dressing

1 cup (235 mL) olive oil
2 cups (475 mL) light vegetable oil
1/3 cup (80 mL) Balsamic vinegar
2/3 cup (155 mL) dry white wine
2 tbsp. (30 mL) lemon juice
2 pinches each minced garlic, chopped basil and sage

- Combine all ingredients, and add salt and pepper to taste. Process or whisk until fully integrated.
- Chill overnight before using.

INSALATA BINDI
Bindi Salad

2 10-oz.(285 g) packets of spinach, stripped of stalks, torn up, rinsed and shaken dry
8 oz. (225 g) salad shrimp, cooked and peeled
1/2 cup (120 mL) mushrooms, thinly sliced
1 cup (235 mL) canned artichoke hearts, drained and sliced
1/2 cup (120 mL) Bindi house dressing (see page 31)
2 tbsp. (30 mL) almond slivers, toasted

- Mix together all ingredients, except dressing and almonds. Toss the dressing through the salad.
- Divide into four salad bowls. Sprinkle with almonds before serving.

INSALATA RADICCHIO
Radicchio Salad

2 heads radicchio lettuce
1/3 cup (80 mL) oil-and-vinegar dressing (see page 29)

- Rinse and dry surface of lettuce heads. Tear apart into bite size pieces.
- Toss through with dressing and serve.

BINDI HOUSE DRESSING

3 cloves garlic, minced
2 tbsp. (30 mL) capers,
   drained and minced
2-1/2 oz. (70 g)
   anchovies, pulped
3/4 cup (175 mL) fresh
   lemon juice
2 dashes Tabasco sauce
1 tsp. (5 mL) Worcester
   sauce
1/2 tsp. (2 mL) freshly
   ground black pepper
2 large egg yolks, well
   beaten
1-3/4 to 2 cups (415-475
   mL) vegetable oil

- Combine in blender or food processor garlic, capers, anchovies, lemon juice, Tabasco and Worcester sauces and pepper. Add egg yolks and process.
- With machine running, pour in oil in slow thin stream. Combine in blender until dressing emulsifies. Makes enough dressing for 4 servings.

$$\boxed{\text{P A S T A}}$$

MANICOTTI DELLA NONNA
Grandmother's Manicotti

15 oz. (425 g) spinach, trimmed and washed

1 lb. (455 g) Ricotta cheese, chopped coarsely

3 oz. (85 g) Parmesan cheese, grated

1-1/2 oz. (45 g) Provolone cheese, chopped finely

2 tbsp. (30 mL) Romano cheese, grated

2 tbsp. (30 mL) fresh lemon juice

1/4 packed cup (60 mL) fresh basil, chopped

1/2 heaped tsp. (2 mL) fresh sage, minced

2 eggs, beaten

Salt and freshly ground black pepper

Ground nutmeg

8 sheets fresh pasta, 6" x 3" (15 cm x 7.5 cm) each

1-1/2 cups (355 mL) Bechamel sauce (see page 37)

- Blanch spinach in boiling water for 30 seconds. Drain and press dry in colander.
- Thoroughly blend or process spinach with cheeses, lemon juice, herbs and eggs, seasoning to taste with salt, pepper and nutmeg.
- Cook pasta in large saucepan of boiling salted water until al dente, cooked but chewy. Drain and allow to cool a little. Put some of spinach-cheese mixture into a piping bag.
- Lay pasta sheets, one at a time, on counter and pipe a quarter of mixture lengthwise down centre of each sheet. Fold sides in to form a tube and set aside, seam side down.
- Cover bottom of baking tray or rectangular sauté dish with half of Bechamel sauce. Cut each of filled pasta tubes in half and arrange in tray, seam side down. Pour

ZUPPA POMODORA AL FINNOCCHIO
Tomato and Fennel Soup
BINDI – PAGE 27

MANICOTTI DELLA NONNA
Grandmother's Manicotti
BINDI – PAGE 32

1-1/2 cups (355 mL)
tomato sauce (see
page 36)
2 oz. (60 g) Parmesan
cheese, grated
Parsley sprigs

remaining Bechamel sauce
on pasta and pour tomato
sauce over this. Sprinkle
with grated Parmesan
cheese.
- Bake in preheated 375°F
(190°C) oven until cheese
begins to brown. Serve at
once with a garnish of
parsley sprigs.

LINGUINE ALLA SALSA DI VONGOLE
Linguine with Red Clam Sauce

1/2 tbsp. (7 mL) olive
oil
1 clove garlic, minced
1 5-oz. (140 g) can baby
clams
1/2 cup (120 mL) dry
white wine
1/2 tsp. (2 mL) dried
oregano
1/2 tsp. (2 mL) dried
thyme
1/2 tsp. (2 mL) dried
rosemary
1 bay leaf

- In sauté pan, cook garlic in
oil until soft. Add liquid
from can of clams, setting
clams aside. Then add wine,
dried herbs, bay leaf, peppercorns and chile. Bring to
a fast simmer and reduce by
half.
- Meanwhile, in a second
saucepan, bring tomato
sauce to a simmer. And in a
third large saucepan, bring
plenty of salted water to the
boil.

1/2 tsp. (2 mL) black peppercorns, coarsely crushed

1/2 tsp (2 mL) crushed chile peppers

3 cups (710 mL) tomato sauce (see page 36)

1 heaped tsp. (5 mL) fresh basil, minced

8-10 oz. (225-285 g) linguine, fresh or dried

- Strain clam juice and wine mixture into tomato sauce and allow to simmer gently. Add linguine to boiling salted water and cook until al dente. Add clams to sauce and warm through.
- Drain cooked pasta and put into a warmed serving dish. Add basil to sauce and toss sauce through linguine. Serve at once.

TORTELLINI ALLA PANNA
Stuffed Pasta in Cream Sauce

4 tbsp. (60 mL) sweet butter

1 medium leek, white part only, finely sliced

1-1/2 cups (355 mL) whipping cream

Salt and freshly ground black pepper

Freshly ground nutmeg

1-1/4 lb. (565 g) fresh tortellini, stuffed with veal or cheese

4-6 oz. (115-170 g) Parmesan cheese, grated

- Melt butter in sauté pan and gently cook leek for 5 minutes. Add cream, bring to a fast simmer and cook until it begins to thicken. Season to taste with salt, pepper and nutmeg, and keep warm.
- In plenty of boiling salted water, cook tortellini until al dente.
- Drain pasta and put into warm serving dish. Mix grated cheese into sauce and pour sauce over tortellini. Serve at once.

PENNE AL OCA AFFUMICATA
Pasta with Smoked Goose

1 tbsp. (15 mL) sweet butter

2 onions, finely chopped

2 cloves garlic, minced

2 cups (475 mL) whipping cream

Salt and freshly ground black pepper

Nutmeg, freshly ground

3 oz. (85 mL) vodka

Dry white wine

Fresh lemon juice

2-4 oz. (60-115 mL) fresh oyster mushrooms, coarsely chopped

3 oz. (85 g) sun-dried tomatoes, julienned

Beurre manié (see page 36)

1-1/2 lbs. (680 g) boneless smoked goose*, julienned

12 oz. (340 g) penne, fresh or dried

- Sauté onion and garlic gently in butter until soft. Meanwhile bring cream to a low simmer in another saucepan.
- Add onion, garlic and butter to cream, season to taste with salt, pepper and nutmeg and cook slowly for 15 minutes.
- Stir vodka into sauce, then a little wine and lemon juice to taste, then mushrooms and tomato. Simmer gently for 5 minutes. Add pieces of buerre manie until sauce begins to thicken, then add julienned goose and warm through. Remove sauce from heat and set aside to cool slightly.
- In plenty of boiling salted water, cook penne until al dente. Drain and turn into warmed serving dish. Toss sauce through pasta and serve warm.

* Obtainable from some specialty butchers or European delicatessan stores. Smoked turkey or chicken may be substituted.

Salsa marinara
Tomato Sauce

3 tbsp. (45 mL) olive oil
2 cloves garlic, minced
2 medium onions,
   finely chopped
1 26-oz. (770 mL) can
   plum tomatoes
2 tbsp. (30 mL) dried
   basil
Salt and freshly
   ground black pepper
Sugar

- Sauté garlic and onion in oil in a large shallow sauté pan until soft. Add tomatoes, breaking up with a spoon, and basil. Bring to a steady simmer, seasoning and adding a little sugar to taste.
- Cook at medium heat, stirring occasionally, until sauce thickens. It should amount to 2-1/2 cups (590 mL).
- Refrigerate in a covered container to use as required. Will keep a week.

Beurre manie

3 tbsp. (45 mL) sweet
   butter, softened
2 tbsp. (30 mL) flour

- Thoroughly work flour into butter to form a thick paste.
- To thicken a simmering sauce, scatter small pieces of beurre manié on surface of sauce, gently rotate pan or stir sauce until it begins to thicken. Keep sauce warm, but do not boil again. Keep remaining beurre manié refrigerated in covered container for later use.

Salsa besciamella
Bechamel Sauce

3 cups (710 mL) milk
4 tbsp. (60 mL) sweet
butter
4 tbsp. (60 mL) flour
1 onion, peeled and
studded with 4 cloves
Salt and freshly
ground white pepper
Nutmeg, freshly
ground

- Warm milk gently in saucepan.
- Melt butter in another saucepan, blend in flour and cook very slowly for 3-4 minutes.
- Slowly add warm milk to roux of butter and flour, bring to a simmer and stir until smooth. Add onion and cook gently for 30 minutes.
- Remove and discard onion. Season sauce to taste with salt, pepper and nutmeg.
- Use as required and refrigerate remainder. Will keep for 5-7 days.

PESCE

RISOTTO AL CALAMARE
Rice with Squid

2 tbsp. (30 mL) sweet butter
1 tsp. (5 mL) crushed chile pepper
1 cup (235 mL) Arborio rice
2-1/2 cups (590 mL) fish stock
1/2 cup (120 mL) dry white wine
2 tbsp. (30 mL) fresh lemon juice
Salt and freshly ground black pepper
1/2 cup (120 mL) cleaned squid, very thinly sliced across
1/2 cup (120 mL) salad shrimp, cooked and shelled
1/2 cup (120 mL) canned plum tomatoes, drained and coarsely chopped
1/4 cup (60 mL) green onions, finely chopped
Parsley sprigs

- In a large shallow sauté pan, gently cook rice in melted butter without browning. Stir in chile peppers. Meanwhile blend fish stock, wine and lemon juice and warm without boiling.
- Add one third (235 mL) of warm stock to rice and allow to simmer very slowly.
- When rice has absorbed most of stock, season to taste with salt and black pepper. Very gently mix in the squid and another third (235 mL) of stock and continue slow cooking.
- When rice has again absorbed stock, carefully blend in shrimp, tomato and onion and adjust seasoning. Rice should be soft outside but firm inside. If not quite cooked, add a little more stock and continue cooking until cooking is complete.
- Turn risotto into warm serving dish, garnish with parsley and serve.

FILETTI DI SOGLIOLA PORTOFINO
Filet of Sole Portofino

Olive or vegetable oil
1 tsp. (5 mL) shallot,
   minced
4 anchovy filets
30 pickled capers,
   drained
2 cups (475 mL)
   tomatoes, peeled,
   seeded and julienned
2 tsp. (10 mL) white
   wine
1 tsp. (5 mL) fresh
   lemon juice
Salt and freshly
   ground black pepper
4 filets lemon sole, 6-8
   oz. (170-225 g) each
1 tbsp. (15 mL) garlic
   butter, softened
Parsley sprigs

- In a sauté pan, cook shallot in a little oil until soft. Pulverize together anchovies and capers and blend well with shallot. Then add tomato slices, wine and lemon juice and reduce briskly, seasoning to taste. When liquid begins to thicken, remove from heat and keep warm.
- Brush sole filets with oil and dust lightly with flour. Broil or panfry for 2-3 minutes each side depending on thickness and brush each filet with garlic butter.
- To serve, spread half sauce on a warm serving platter, arrange filets on sauce, then garnish with remaining sauce and parsley sprigs.

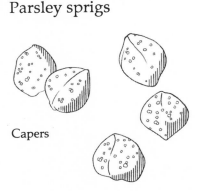

Capers

SALMONE AL FORNO
Baked Salmon

4 filets of salmon, 6-8 oz. (170-225 g) each

2 tbsp. (30 mL) garlic, minced

1/2 cup (120 mL) vegetable oil

Salt and freshly ground black pepper

2 tbsp. (30 mL) sweet butter

1 tbsp. (15 mL) shallot, minced

1 cup (235 mL) whipping cream

3 tbsp. (45 mL) raspberry or tarragon vinegar

- Arrange filets in a shallow baking tray. Sprinkle with garlic. Pour oil over fish. Season to taste. Bake in preheated 375°F (190°C) oven for 5-6 minutes, depending on thickness of filets.

- Meanwhile cook shallot in butter in a sauté pan until soft. Add cream and simmer briskly until liquid begins to thicken, then add vinegar and cook a few minutes more. Season to taste, remove from heat and keep warm.

- Arrange filets on warm serving platter and garnish with sauce.

| CARNE E POLLAME |

MANZO ALLA BOSCAIOLA
Stuffed Beef Tenderloin

4 thick filets of beef
  tenderloin, about 8
  oz. (225 g) each
3 tbsp.(45 mL)
  vegetable oil or 3
  tbsp. (45 mL) sweet
  butter
1-1/4 cups (285 mL)
  chopped cooked
  spinach
2 shallots, minced
6 oz. (170 g) button
  mushrooms,
  quartered
1 bunch green onions,
  chopped finely
1 clove garlic, minced
1 heaped tbsp. (15 mL)
  each chopped fresh
  rosemary and thyme
Salt and freshly
  ground black pepper
5 oz. (140 g) hazelnuts,
  toasted and coarsely
  crushed
3 cups (710 mL) tomato
  sauce (see page 36)

- Cut a pocket part way
  through each filet from the
  edge. Sear outsides of filets
  in a little hot oil or butter.
- Combine remaining
  ingredients, except tomato
  sauce, as a stuffing,
  seasoning to taste. Stuff
  each filet.
- Put stuffed filets in a
  shallow baking tray with a
  little oil or butter. Bake in a
  preheated 400°F (205°C)
  oven, basting occasionally,
  to required tenderness.
- Meanwhile bring tomato
  sauce to simmer.
- Pour sauce into a warm
  serving platter and arrange
  filets on top.

FILETTINI DUE PEPI
Filets of Baby Beef

4 filets of baby beef
  tenderloin, each
  about 6 oz. (170 g)
Flour
Salt and freshly
  ground black pepper
Vegetable oil
2/3 cup (155 mL) brown
  veal or beef stock
4 tbsp. (60 mL)
  whipping cream
1 tsp. (5 mL) each of
  pickled green and
  pink peppercorns,
  drained
1 tbsp. (15 mL) shallot,
  minced
2 tbsp. (30 mL) garlic
  butter
2 oz. (60 mL) brandy

- Cut each filet across in three slices and beat out very thin with flat side of a cleaver. Lightly flour each slice and season to taste. Quickly sauté each slice in a little hot oil, 1-2 minutes each side, and keep warm in oven.

- When meat is cooked, pour stock into same sauté pan and loosen any sediment from bottom. Reduce over high heat. When sauce begins to thicken, add cream, peppercorns and shallot. Blend briefly over low heat, then stir in garlic butter.

- Pour most of sauce onto a warm serving platter. Arrange beef slices on top. Pour remainder of sauce over meat, flame with brandy and serve at once with appropriate side vegetables.

PICCATA DI POLLO AL LIMONE
Breast of Chicken in Lemon

4 boneless breasts of
chicken
4 tbsp. (60 mL) olive oil
1 level tsp. (5 mL) each
of minced fresh
rosemary, thyme
and oregano
1 tbsp. (15 mL) black
peppercorns, coarsely
crushed
2 tbsp. (30 mL) sweet
butter
2 tbsp. (30 mL) shallot,
minced
6 tbsp. (90 mL) dry
white wine
4 tbsp. (60 mL) fresh
lemon juice
Salt
Parsley sprigs

- Divide each chicken breast into 4 thin slices.
- Combine oil, herbs and peppercorns, pour over chicken and marinate at room temperature for at least an hour.
- Remove chicken from marinade and quickly fry slices in hot dry sauté pan for 2 minutes each. Set aside on warm serving platter.
- Briefly sauté shallot in a little butter. Add wine and lemon juice and reduce over high heat, seasoning to taste, then stir in remaining butter.
- Pour sauce over chicken slices and garnish with parsley. Serve with fresh vegetables.

LOMBATA D'AGNELLO AL FORNO
Roast Loin of Lamb

4 boneless slices of loin of lamb, 6-8 oz. (170-225 g) each (order specially from butcher)

Salt and freshly ground black pepper

1/2 cup (120 mL) olive oil

1 tbsp. (15 mL) shallot, minced

1/2 cup (120 mL) lamb or veal stock

1/2 cup (120 mL) red wine

2 tbsp. (30 mL) fresh mint, chopped

2 tbsp. (30 mL) sweet butter

- Season lamb slices and sear both sides in hot oil. Roast in preheated 400°F (205°C) oven to desired tenderness.
- Remove cooked meat to warm serving platter. Add a little oil to roasting pan and sauté shallot on top of stove until soft. Add stock and wine and bring to a rapid boil, scraping free any meat residue from bottom of pan. When sauce begins to thicken, season to taste, stir in mint and butter and cook for 2 more minutes.
- Pour sauce around meat and serve at once with suitable side vegetables.

$\boxed{\text{D O L C E}}$

Torta di frutta fresca
Fresh Fruit Tart

---

1 lb. (455 g) chilled
Linzer dough (see
page 47)
2 egg whites, beaten
2/3 cup (225 mL) crème
fraîche (see below)
1 to 1-1/2 cups (235-355
mL) fresh berries
(blueberries, straw-
berries, raspberries
or seedless grapes)
Icing sugar

- Roll out pastry and line bottom and sides of 10" (25 cm) shallow pie tray with removable bottom. Brush surface of pastry with egg white and allow to dry.
- Bake piecrust in preheated 350°F (175°C) oven until brown. Allow to cool completely.
- Just before serving, spread bottom of crust with crème fraîche and arrange berries in concentric circles. Remove from pie tray, sprinkle lightly with sugar and serve, cut in wedges.

Creme fraiche

3-1/2 cups (830 mL)
whipping cream
1 cup (235 mL) sugar
1/2 cup (120 mL) fresh
lemon juice
Pinch of salt
Vanilla essence

- Thoroughly whisk together all ingredients in a bowl, flavoring to taste with vanilla. Cover and leave at room temperature for 24 hours.
- Stir mixture well, cover again and refrigerate for another 24 hours before using.

TORTA CIOCCOLATA CON NOCI
Walnut Chocolate Tart

1 lb. (455 g) chilled
  Linzer dough (see
  page 47)
2 egg whites, beaten
8 oz. (225 mL) corn
  syrup
1/2 cup (120 g) sugar
5 oz. (140 g) dark cook-
  ing chocolate, melted
3 eggs, beaten
Vanilla essence
8 oz. (225 g) walnut
  pieces

- Roll out pastry and line bottom and sides of 10" (25 cm) shallow pie tray with removable bottom. Brush surface of pastry with egg white and allow to dry.
- Bake piecrust in preheated 350°F (175°C) oven until it begins to set. Then remove and put aside.
- Thoroughly mix together corn syrup, sugar and melted chocolate. Then blend in beaten eggs and vanilla to taste. Finally add walnut pieces and mix well.
- Pour chocolate and nut mixture into half-baked piecrust and spread out carefully. Bake in preheated 350°F (175°C) oven for 25-30 minutes. Remove, carefully take out of pie tray and allow to cool slightly before removing from tray to serving plate. Serve cut in wedges.

LINZER DOUGH

1 cup (235 mL) sweet
  butter, softened
1 cup (235 mL) icing
  sugar
1 egg
2 cups (475 mL) pastry
  flour
3/4 cup (175 mL) cookie
  crumbs
1-1/2 cups (355 mL)
  ground almonds or
  hazelnuts
Pinch of salt
1/2 tsp. (2 mL)
  cinnamon

- Whisk butter until creamy.
  Add sugar and whisk until
  fluffy, then incorporate egg.
- Mix in flour, crumbs, ground
  nuts, salt and cinnamon to
  form a dough.
- Chill in covered container
  until required.

Bindi Ristorante Recommended Wines

BIANCHI
Soave Anselmi
Riesling Ca'Bolani
Cortese Piemontese

ROSSI
Salice Salentino
Refosco Nostrano
Vino Nobile di
  Montepulciano

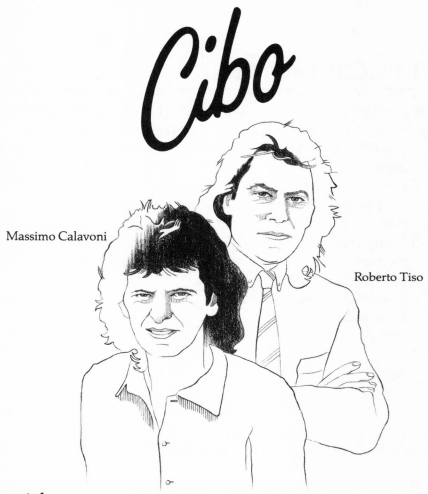

Cibo

Massimo Calavoni

Roberto Tiso

*N*ot only was Cibo one of the Italian pioneers in making an open kitchen a feature of its decor, but it also played a leading role in establishing the particular stretch of Yonge Street on which it stands as an enclave of fine and adventurous dining.

Set on the border of Rosedale's residential affluence and within easy reach of both the Annex and Bloor Street, its early success was not a great surprise. The area had some tradition in dining out: a few blocks to the north *The Ports Of Call* had established itself as the place to go among a more conservative earlier generation of well-off diners.

For reasons somewhat too complicated to be explored here, the Toronto generation of the early 1980s, eager to eat well and stylishly, developed a preference for modern Italian cuisine, lightly prepared fresh ingredients presented with panache. The two partners who launched Cibo Ristorante in 1982, if dissimilar in personality, both came from Northern Italy, the cradle of that cucina nuova.

Roberto Tiso seems to possess the flair for stage-managing a restaurant where an almost theatrical air of excitement must be provoked; his partner, Massimo Calavoni, though apparently shyer, carries with him the intensity needed to generate much of that excitement from the activities in the open kitchen which he rules. There persists, whether justified or not, an expectation that high emotion must closely attend what Italians do. Though service at Cibo is always smartly attentive – a necessity in so busy an establishment – there is about it what one faithful customer describes as "an undercurrent of beguiling anarchy". Since its two owners are almost the only native Italians involved in its running, they must be credited with inciting that casual attractive verve.

But its regular patrons, too, are owed some credit for the persistent success and sense of occasion of the restaurant. It is almost impossible to gauge all the factors that govern public response to a new dining place, but, for whatever reasons, Cibo's initial popularity began to soar within two days of its opening.

Early reviews of its cuisine were generally laudatory.

Mentions of the celebrated who flocked there to see and be seen were flatteringly frequent in newspaper columns. The pressure on the staff was intense, but not fatally so. Inevitably, the prompt success of Cibo encouraged emulation, not only in other modern Italian establishments elsewhere in the city, but also, eventually, in several other competitors with fashionable gourmet ambitions in the immediate locality.

As is often the case, the competitive emulation has proved in the long run to be beneficial to Cibo. The restaurant has been relieved of the stress of its high celebrity without being relieved of the support of its more faithful clientele.

In the Northern Italian style, Cibo relies much on fresh fish and vegetables, presenting those ingredients and the meat it offers decoratively and lightly cooked. A broad and inventive range of pasta dishes, frequently augmented, is possibly the most striking feature of the cuisine.

An expanse of window lends the place an ambience as light and airy as its cuisine and fits well with the overt energy with which it runs. The central sit-up bar, the bustling open kitchen near the entrance and, in summer, the patio overlooking the restless traffic of Yonge Street, all contribute to the variety and excitement expected as essentially Italian contributions to living.

CIBO RISTORANTE, 1055 Yonge Street. Telephone: 921-2166.
Open every day (except December 24-26 and January 1) for lunch from noon to 3 p.m. and for dinner from 6 to 11.30 p.m. Fully licensed. Major cards accepted.
Reservations recommended.

$$\boxed{\text{A N T I P A S T I}}$$

COZZE IN BRODETTO
Mussels in Sauce

2 lbs. (1 kg) fresh
  cultured mussels
3 oz. (85 mL) dry white
  wine
1 tbsp. (15 mL) olive oil
3 cloves garlic, finely
  minced
1 tbsp. (15 mL) each
  celery, carrot and
  onion cut in fine
  julienne slices
2 cups (475 mL) tomato
  sauce (see page 64)
Salt and freshly
  ground black pepper
1 piled tbsp. (15 mL)
  fresh chopped basil

— Scrub and remove beard
  from mussels, discarding
  any with open shells. Put in
  a heavy pan with wine,
  cover and cook over medium
  heat for 3-4 minutes until all
  shells are open.
— Briefly sauté garlic and
  other vegetables in oil, add
  tomato sauce and bring to
  boil, seasoning to taste.
  Strain in liquid and wine
  from mussels and blend.
— Pour sauce into serving dish,
  pile mussels in shells on top,
  garnish with basil and serve.

MOZZARELLA POMODORI E PROSCIUTTO CALDI
Baked Cheese with Tomato and Prosciutto

4 bocconcini (rounds of
  mozzarella cheese)*
4 slices of vine tomato
4 leaves fresh basil
4 thin slices prosciutto
3 oz. (85 mL) dry white
  wine
3 tbsp. (45 mL) sweet
  butter
Chopped parsley

* Obtainable in Italian or
gourmet cheese stores.

- Lay a tomato slice on each round of cheese, top with a basil leaf and wrap in prosciutto. Arrange cheese packages, fold side down, in an ovenproof serving dish, sprinkle with wine and dot with butter. Bake in a preheated oven at 400°F (205°C) until cheese begins to melt.
- Garnish with parsley and serve immediately.

GAMBERI FRA DIAVOLO
Shrimp Fra Diavolo

12-18 medium shrimp
  (about 1 lb. or 455 g),
  cleaned and deveined
Vegetable oil
2 tbsp. (30 mL) sweet
  butter
1 clove garlic, finely
  minced
1 oz. (30 mL) brandy

- Partly cut through shrimp lengthwise, and open flat in butterfly shape. Sauté in a little hot oil for 2-3 minutes, drain off oil, add butter and cook garlic briefly. Flambé shrimp with brandy,then add cream, tomato sauce and seasoning to taste.

2/3 cup (155 mL)
  whipping cream
2 tbsp. (30 mL) tomato
  sauce (see page 64)
Salt and freshly
  ground black pepper
Pinch cayenne pepper

- Simmer for a few minutes, then remove shrimp to warm serving platter and reduce sauce over high heat until it begins to thicken.
- Pour sauce over shrimp, sprinkle with cayenne pepper and serve very hot.

FRITTATA
Open-Face Omelette

3 tbsp. (45 mL) clarified
  butter
12 eggs, well beaten
Salt and freshly
  ground black pepper
8 slices lean bacon,
  cooked crisp
2 oz. (60 mL) Swiss
  cheese, e.g., Gruyere,
  thinly sliced
Fresh basil, chopped
1 tbsp. (15 mL)
  Parmesan cheese,
  grated

- Heat butter in shallow sauté dish, pour in eggs, stir over low heat, seasoning to taste, until cooked through but still soft. Remove from heat, arrange bacon on top, cover with a layer of Swiss cheese and scatter with basil to taste.
- Bake in preheated oven at 400°F (205°C) until cheese begins to melt. Remove, garnish with Parmesan and serve, dividing into wedges.

INSALATE

INSALATA DI RADICCHIO E LATTUGA VERDE
Mixed Salad

1 head Boston lettuce
1 head radicchio
  lettuce
3/4 cup (175 mL) virgin
  olive oil
1/4 cup (60 mL)
  balsamic vinegar
Salt and freshly
  ground black pepper
Chopped parsley

- Tear up both heads of lettuce, discarding any coarse stalks. Wash thoroughly and shake dry.
- Thoroughly mix together oil and vinegar, seasoning to taste and toss well through the lettuce.
- Serve garnished with parsley.

INSALATA DI FARFALLE FREDDE
Cold Butterfly Pasta Salad

7 oz. (200 g) farfalle
  (butterfly-shaped)
  pasta
3-1/2 oz. (100 g) fresh
  Fontina cheese
8 cherry tomatoes
1/2 hot banana pepper,
  cored
Fresh basil, chopped
4 tbsp. (60 mL) olive oil
Juice of 1 lemon
Salt and freshly
  ground black pepper

- In a large saucepan of salted boiling water, cook pasta until al dente, cooked but chewy. Drain and allow to cool.
- Dice the cheese, cut tomatoes in half, julienne the banana pepper. Mix these ingredients with oil, lemon juice and basil, seasoning to taste.
- Mix cheese and vegetables into pasta and serve.

INSALATA DI POMODORI E CIPOLLINI
Tomato and Onion Salad

4 small vine tomatoes
1 medium red onion
4 green onions
4 cloves garlic, finely
  minced
1/4 cup (60 mL) red
  wine vinegar
Juice of 1 lemon
Salt and freshly
  ground black pepper
3/4 cup (175 mL) virgin
  olive oil
1 large head Boston
  lettuce

- Slice tomatoes in eighths, julienne red onion and chop green onion finely.
- In stainless steel or ceramic bowl, mix garlic, vinegar, lemon juice and seasoning to taste. Still whisking, thoroughly incorporate the oil.
- Gently toss dressing through onion and tomato. Serve in bowl lined with washed and dried lettuce leaves.

PASTA

CONCHIGLIE BUONE
Noodles with Prosciutto

1 lb. (455 g) conchiglie
noodles (shell-shaped
pasta)
4 tbsp. (60 mL) sweet
butter
5 oz. (140 g) prosciutto,
julienned
8 oz. (225 g) fresh
green peas
2 oz. (60 mL) vodka
3/4 cup (175 mL)
tomato sauce (see
page 64)
3/4 cup (175 mL)
whipping cream
Salt and freshly
ground black pepper
Parmesan cheese,
grated

- In plenty of boiling salted water, cook noodles al dente. Drain and keep warm.
- Sauté prosciutto in butter, stirring to prevent sticking. Blanch peas in boiling water for 2 minutes, drain and add to prosciutto with vodka. Reduce vodka over medium heat. Add tomato sauce and cream, seasoning to taste, and cook for 3-4 minutes.
- In a warmed serving dish, mix sauce through noodles. Serve sprinkled with Parmesan.

FETTUCCINE "ARLECCHINO"

3 tbsp. (45 mL) sweet
butter
3 tbsp. (45 mL) olive oil
1 small caulifower,
broken into florets

- Heat butter and oil in large skillet. Add all vegetables and sauté over medium heat, stirring gently to avoid any burning. Add wine and

1 head broccoli, broken into florets

3-4 oz. (85-115 g) snow peas, trimmed

2 oz. (60 g) green beans, trimmed and halved

1 small zucchini, julienned

1 small eggplant, unpeeled, cut in small cubes

16 spears young asparagus

1 red bell pepper, cored, seeded and julienned

1 green bell pepper, cored, seeded and julienned

1 medium vine tomato, seeded and cubed

6 tbsp. (90 mL) dry white wine

1 cup (225 mL) whipping cream

Salt and freshly ground black pepper

1 lb. (455 g) fettuccine, fresh or dried

1/2 cup (120 mL) Parmesan cheese, grated

let simmer until liquid has evaporated. Add cream and season to taste.

■ Meanwhile, in a large saucepan, bring plenty of salted water to a rapid boil. Add fettuccine and, stirring occasionally, cook until al dente. Drain thoroughly and combine with vegetables in a warmed serving dish, adding Parmesan and mixing well. Serve at once.

MACCHERONCINI
AL GORGONZOLA
Small Macaroni with Gorgonzola

14 oz. (395 g) small
  macaroni
7 oz. (200 g)
  Gorgonzola cheese
5/6 cup (200 mL)
  whipping cream
2 oz. (60 mL) Bourbon
  whisky
3 tbsp. (45 mL)
  Parmesan cheese,
  grated
Salt and freshly
  ground black pepper

- In plenty of boiling salted water, cook pasta al dente. Drain and keep warm.
- In a heavy saucepan, melt Gorgonzola, then blend in cream, whisky, Parmesan and seasoning to taste. Continue stirring until sauce begins to thicken. Blanch broccoli in boiling water for 2 minutes and break into florets.
- Combine pasta and sauce in a warmed serving dish. Garnish with florets of broccoli and serve.

SPAGHETTI AL AGLIO, OLIO E PEPERONCINO
Spaghetti with Garlic, Oil and Hot Pepper

7 oz. (200 g) spaghetti
  or linguine, fresh or
  dried
1/2 cup (120 mL) olive
  oil
4 cloves garlic, finely
  minced
2 fresh hot banana
  peppers, cored,
  seeded and julienned
  (or 2 pinches crushed
  chile pepper)
Salt and freshly
  ground black pepper
Chopped parsley

- Cook pasta in plenty of boiling salted water until al dente, and drain thoroughly.
- Meanwhile, over high heat, sauté garlic and peppers in oil. Add pasta to skillet. Sauté and mix until well covered in sauce, seasoning to taste.
- Turn pasta into warmed serving dish and garnish with parsley before serving.

FUSILLI MARINARA
Seafood Spirals

---

14 oz. (395 g) fusilli
 (spiral-shaped pasta)
1 lb. (455 g) cultured
 mussels
1 tbsp. (15 mL) olive oil
3 cloves garlic, finely
 minced
2 oz. (60 g) baby shrimp,
 cooked and shelled
2 oz. (60 g) canned baby
 clams, drained
1/2 cup (120 mL) baby
 squid, cleaned, cooked
 and sliced
3 tbsp. (45 mL) dry
 white wine
3/4 cup (175 mL) toma-
 to sauce (see page 64)
Salt and freshly ground
 black pepper
Chopped
 parsley

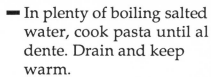

Fusilli

— In plenty of boiling salted water, cook pasta until al dente. Drain and keep warm.
— Scrub and beard mussels, discarding any that remain open. In a little water, cook over medium heat in a covered saucepan for 3-4 minutes until all shells open.
— In large skillet, sauté the garlic and other seafood in oil for 3-4 minutes, then add drained mussels in shells. Turn up heat, pour in wine and flambé. Mix in tomato sauce, warm through over medium heat and season to taste.
— Mix sauce through pasta in warmed serving dish. Grind some more black pepper over it, garnish with parsley and serve.

$$\boxed{\text{P E S C E}}$$

SALMONE CITRICO
Salmon with Citrus Sauce

4 salmon steaks, 7-8
  oz. (200-225 g) each
1 cup (235 mL) dry
  white wine
1 lemon, 1 small
  orange, and 1 lime,
  each halved and
  thinly sliced
3 tbsp. (45 mL) sweet
  butter
1 tbsp. (15 mL)
  whipping cream
Salt and freshly
  ground black pepper

■ Preheat oven to 350°F
  (175°C). Arrange steaks in
  shallow sauté pan and pour
  wine over them. Bake in
  oven for 5-7 minutes,
  depending on thickness,
  basting occasionally.
■ Remove steaks and keep
  warm in serving dish. Reduce wine to one-third over
  high heat. Add sliced fruit,
  butter, cream and seasoning
  to taste and heat through
  thoroughly. Pour liquid over
  fish and arrange citrus slices
  as garnish before serving
  with fresh vegetables.

GAMBERI NOCETO
Shrimp with Nuts

12 tiger shrimp,
  shelled, deveined,
  with tails left on
Salt and freshly
  ground black pepper
4 tbsp. (60 mL)
  vegetable oil

■ In heavy skillet turn shrimp,
  seasoned to taste, in oil over
  high heat for 2-3 minutes.
■ Drain off excess oil, add
  Cointreau and flambé. Add
  nuts, onions and cream and
  cook for 2 more minutes.

4 oz. (115 mL) 6 tbsp.
  Cointreau
16 lichee nuts, canned
  or fresh
12 Brazil nuts
4 green onions, finely
  chopped
1 cup (235 mL)
  whipping cream
(90 mL) sweet butter
1 head radicchio
  lettuce
Zest thinly pared from
  1 orange

Remove shrimp to warmed
serving dish, reduce sauce
until it begins to thicken.
Blend in butter and remove
from heat.

— Arrange shrimp on bed of
radicchio leaves, pour on
sauce, garnish with orange
zest and serve with fresh
vegetables of choice.

SALSA DI POMODORO
Tomato Sauce

2 tbsp. (30 mL)
vegetable oil
2 tbsp. (30 mL) sweet
butter
1 small onion, finely
chopped
2-1/4 cups (525 mL)
canned plum
tomatoes
1 clove garlic, chopped
1 small carrot,
scrubbed
1/2 stalk celery
2 fresh basil leaves
1 branch of fresh
rosemary
1 bay leaf
Salt and freshly
ground black pepper

- In a large shallow pan,
sauté onion in oil and butter
until it turns translucent.
Add tomatoes and garlic and
bring to a slow simmer.
- Tie together carrot, celery,
basil, rosemary and bay leaf
as a bouquet garni and add
to the sauce.
- Cook for about 25 minutes,
whisking occasionally, until
sauce becomes smooth and
thick. Season to taste.
- Use as required. Sauce may
be refrigerated in a closed
container until needed. It
will keep 7 days.

COZZE IN BRODETTO
Mussels in Sauce
CIBO – PAGE 52

FRITTATA
Open-Face Omelette
CIBO – PAGE 54

CONCHIGLIE BUONE
Noodles with Prosciutto
CIBO – PAGE 57

MINESTRA PEPERONI FREDDO
Chilled Roast Pepper Soup
ORSO – PAGE 82

| CARNE E POLLAME |

VITELLO ALLE PERE
Veal with Pears

4 tbsp. (60 mL) sweet
  butter
1 tbsp. (15 mL)
  vegetable oil
4 veal scallopine, about
  6 oz. (170 g) each
2 oz. (60 mL) Strega
  (Italian liqueur)
1/2 cup (120 mL) demi-
  glace (see page 66)
1 tbsp. (15 mL)
  whipping cream
Salt and freshly
  ground black pepper
2 Bartlett pears,
  peeled, halved and
  cored

- Heat 1 tbsp. (15 mL) butter and oil in heavy skillet. Divide each scallopine into three and beat out very thin with flat of a cleaver.
- Over medium high heat, quickly sauté scallopine, at most 2 minutes each side. Pour off excess cooking fat and flambé with Strega. Remove scallopine to serving platter and keep warm.
- Add demi-glace and cream to skillet and reduce slightly over high heat, seasoning to taste, then stir in rest of butter and do not reheat. Blanch pear halves in boiling water for 1 minute. Thinly slice each half pear lengthwise and at an angle, from bulb end but not all the way to stem end. Arrange each half pear decoratively inside each set of 3 scallopine, over which some of sauce has been poured. Serve with side vegetables of choice.

MANZO AL FUNGHETTO
Beef Tenderloin with Mushrooms

1 tbsp. (15 mL)
vegetable oil
24 oz. (640 g) beef
tenderloin cut into 8
slices
1/4 cup (60 mL) brandy
1/4 cup (60 mL) red
wine
12 small mushrooms
1 porcini mushroom,
fresh if possible
12 fresh chantrelles
4 oz. (115 g) packet
fresh enoki
mushrooms
Salt and freshly
ground black pepper
3/4 cup (175 mL)
whipping cream
1/4 cup (60 mL) demi-
glace*
3 tbsp. (45 mL) sweet
butter

- Heat oil in heavy skillet. Sauté tenderloin slices on both sides to desired tenderness. Pour off excess oil and flambé meat with brandy. Remove tenderloin to warm serving platter.
- Add wine to skillet and reduce by half, then add mushrooms, seasoning to taste, and cook for 3-4 minutes. Add cream, demi-glace and butter and reduce over medium heat. Pour sauce over beef and serve with appropriate side vegetables.

Porcini (cepes)

* DEMI-GLACE: Normally this is a specially-made concentrate of meat juices, heavy in flavor and texture, used to finish sauces or glaze the surface of entrees. A clear meat or poultry stock, reduced over medium heat until it begins to thicken, can be used as a substitute.

SCALLOPINE DI VITELLO BOSCAIOLA
Veal Scallopine

6 tbsp. (90 mL)
  vegetable oil
3 tbsp. (45 mL) sweet
  butter
1 medium onion, thinly
  sliced
1 red and 1 yellow
  pepper, each cored
  and julienned
2 medium vine
  tomatoes, peeled,
  seeded and cubed
16 button mushroom
  caps, quartered
1/4 cup (60 mL) dry
  white wine
Salt and freshly
  ground black pepper
Flour
12 veal scallopine,
  about 2 oz. (60 g)
  each, beaten thin

- In a skillet, in half the oil and butter, sauté onion and peppers for 3-4 minutes. Increase heat, add tomatoes, mushrooms and wine and cook for 2-3 minutes more, seasoning to taste.
- In another skillet, heat remaining oil and butter. Lightly flour scallopine and sauté 2-3 minutes each side. Pour sauce into a warmed serving platter, arrange scallopine on sauce and serve with vegetables of choice.

PETTO DI POLLO ALLA SALVIA
Chicken Breasts with Sage

8 half chicken breasts
Flour
2 eggs, well beaten
1/2 cup (120 mL)
  breadcrumbs
1/2 cup (120 mL)
  Parmesan chesse,
  grated
Salt and freshly
  ground black pepper
2 tbsp. (30 mL)
  vegetable oil
1/2 cup (120 mL)
  Martini & Rossi
  white vermouth
6 tbsp. (90 mL) sweet
  butter
4 sprigs fresh sage

- Lightly dust chicken breast with flour, dip in egg, then coat in mixture of breadcrumbs, cheese and seasoning to taste. Heat oil in heavy skillet.
- Sauté chicken in oil over medium heat until tender and lightly browned, then remove and keep warm.
- Add vermouth to skillet and bring to boil. Add butter and sage sprigs and stir until butter is blended.
- Arrange chicken breasts on serving platter. Pour sauce over them and garnish with sage sprigs. Serve with fresh vegetables of choice.

$$\boxed{\text{D O L C E}}$$

SPUMA DI LEMONE
Lemon Mousse

Half envelope of
  gelatine
2 tbsp. (30 mL) cold
  water
2 egg yolks
6 tbsp. (90 mL) sugar
1/4 cup (60 mL) fresh
  lemon juice
1-1/2 tbsp. (20 mL)
  grated lemon zest
2 egg whites
4 tbsp. (60 mL) sugar
1/2 cup (120 mL)
  whipping cream

- Sprinkle gelatine on cold water to soften.
- In a stainless steel or ceramic bowl set over simmering water, whisk egg yolks, 6 tbsp. (90 mL) sugar and lemon juice until bubbles form and mixture begins to thicken. Remove from heat, combine with dissolved gelatine and lemon rind. Chill until mixture begins to set.
- Meanwhile whip egg whites and remaining sugar until stiff. Also whip cream until stiff. Fold egg whites, then cream, into lemon mixture.
- Chill again, allowing time for mousse to set before serving.

FRAGOLE AL VINO ROSSO
Strawberries in Red Wine

1 pint (0.5 L) fresh
  strawberries
Juice of 1 lemon
2 tbsp. (30 mL) sugar
3/4 cup (175 mL) red
  wine

- Pit and wash strawberries. Cut in half and mix with lemon and sugar in a stainless steel or ceramic bowl. Refrigerate for 5 minutes.
- Mix red wine through berries and serve.

Cibo Recommended Wines

BIANCHI
Cortese del Piemonte (Selezione 1985)**
Torre di Giano (Lungarotti 1985)
Pinot Grigio (Collavini. Grave del Friuli 1985)

ROSSI
Pinot Nero del Veneto (Ponte 1979)
Ghemme 1979 (Umberto Fiore)**
Masi Campo Fiorin (1978 Verona)

** *Private imports*

Orso

John Maxwell

Roland Richter

_T_he idea of Orso was inspired by a trip through Italy
in 1983 shared by the American restauranteur Joe
Allen and his Toronto partner John Maxwell. What they
conceived was a series of Italian-styled restaurants providing the same quality of service and cuisine already
offered by Joe Allen establishments in New York, Toronto
and London, but breaking with the then fashionable bias
towards Northern Italian food by offering also some of
the more attractive elements of Southern and Central

Italian cuisine; in effect an amalgam of the usually diverse regional characteristics of Italian cooking.

The first incarnation of the Orso name was in a converted New York brownstone in 1984. Its initial intimations of success spurred efforts to open a second Orso in Toronto. Chance rather than firm intention eventually provided a building for the Canadian restaurant not more than a hundred yards away from the already established Toronto Joe Allen restaurant.

The two-storey building at 105 John Street, originally a home but in 1984 shared by a couple of small businesses, was not only too small but was also close to structural collapse. Nonetheless John Maxwell did perceive about the place a foreshadowing of the character he sought. Reinforcement and sandblasting, along with the addition of a veranda in front and a two-storey wing with a roof-level patio behind, has resulted quite magically in an apparently antique building that would not seem out of place in a small venerable Italian city.

In reality, this Orso, larger than the New York original, stands together with Joe Allen almost at the hub of the most rapidly burgeoning restaurant locality in Toronto. The district's initial growth was owed to the Royal Alexandra Theatre, the CN Tower and the new Roy Thomson Concert Hall nearby. It was further encouraged by the opening of a vast new Convention Centre to the south and is now greatly accelerated by the prospective building of a CBC broadcast centre and the grandiose Domed Stadium in the vicinity.

Such massive activity seems somehow quite out of keeping with the sense of warm and intimate grace that

John Maxwell and his executive chef, Roland Richter, have managed to conjure from their rescued building. But their magic as culinary illusionists depends on much much more than the mere set within which they perform.

A precise lively man, John Maxwell exudes a sense of alert awareness. While the disciplinary mechanics are kept soothingly invisible, one can appreciate that he must run a very tight ship to ensure such elegant and carefree voyages for his clientele.

His attention to detail seems flawless: the choice of pastels exactly enhances the scale of the restaurant's interior. The separation of the tables is exactly and comfortably right for the balance of privacy and conviviality sought. The prompt yet unpushy attentiveness of the front of house staff seems instinctive. And as reminders of the earthy rustic sources of Italian cuisine, as each course is served, there are the vivid pastoral tints of Orso's specially designed plates and bowls.

If Maxwell is the captain of Orso, his chief engineer is Roland Richter, who commands its cleverly sited open kitchen. Born in southern Germany, the executive chef was obviously influenced by the Bavarian liking for rich and colorful food.

He seems too young and slim and fit for such onerous responsibility in the kitchen, but en route to Joe Allen and subsequently Orso, he had schooled himself in Stuttgart and London not only in the practicalities of restaurant cooking but also in the scientific essentials of nutrition. The confidence drawn from such knowledge, devoted to providing fine food, seems to have endowed him also with an enviable calm and a charming sense of humor.

While how food is served is a most important concern
at Orso, what is served is accorded the same scrupulous
attention. The Southern Italian dishes included in the
menu bear no resemblance to the ponderous Italianate
concoctions thought suitable for North Americans until
quite recently. Southern Italy's reputation for heavy and
crudely flavored food was to a large extent unjustified
and, as John Maxwell points out, South cuisine too has
joined the move towards inventive lightness in the recent
past.

Adventurous originality firmly based on Italian culinary sensibility is always evident in the ever-changing
variety of antipasti, pasta and pizza offered on the Orso
menu. Nor are the main courses ever wanting in delight-
ful ingenuity.

The impression imposed is that everything at Orso, from seasoning to welcoming, from freshness of ingredients to shine of cutlery, has been given the same scrupulous attention. The result is exceptional pleasure.

ORSO, 105 John Street. Telephone: 596-1989. Open for lunch and dinner Monday to Saturday from 11.30 a.m. to midnight. Fully licensed. Major cards accepted. Reservations recommended.

$$\boxed{\text{A N T I P A S T I}}$$

RADICCHIO E FUNGHI AI FERRI
Grilled Radicchio and Oyster Mushrooms

---

1 head radicchio
8 oz. (225 g) oyster
  mushrooms
1 cup (235 mL) virgin
  olive oil
2 piled tbsp. (30 mL)
  Italian parsley, finely
  chopped
2 lemons, halved
Salt and freshly
  ground black pepper

— Radicchio grows so tightly that it needs no washing. Peel off and discard outer layer of leaves, then cut head into quarters. Put in a bowl and saturate with oil, allowing some to soak between layers of leaves. Shake off excess.

— Wipe mushrooms with damp paper towel. Cut into pieces about 3" (7.5 cm) long and 1-1/2" (4 cm) wide, allowing four pieces per serving. Coat mushrooms thoroughly with olive oil.

— Arrange radicchio quarters, flat sides down, on a hot charcoal or gas grill. After 90 seconds, turn quarters onto other flat sides. Then place mushroom pieces on grill. After a further 90 seconds, turn radicchio quarters onto rounded sides and turn over mushroom pieces. Season radicchio and mushroom with coarse salt and pepper.

- After a final 90 seconds or so on the grill, remove nicely charred portions and divide among 4 plates. Garnish with chopped parsley and serve with halves of lemon.

COZZE CON PANCHETTA, FINOCCHIO E PANNA
Mussels with Bacon, Fennel and Cream

1-1/2 lbs. (680 g) cultured mussels
1 tbsp. (15 mL) sweet butter
1/2 bulb fresh fennel, finely diced
4 oz. (115 g) panchetta (cured unsmoked Italian bacon), diced
3/4 cup (175 mL) whipping cream
4 tbsp. (60 mL) dry white wine
6 shallots, finely chopped
Salt and freshly ground black pepper
Chopped parsley

- Scrub and beard mussels, discarding any that stay open.
- Melt butter in shallow steel sauté pan and sauté fennel and shallots for 3 minutes. Add panchetta and black pepper and continue to cook until fennel is tender.
- Add mussels and wine. When mussels begin to open, add cream. Cover, bring to boil and cook for 2-3 minutes. All mussels should be open.
- Remove from heat, take out opened mussels in shells and arrange on a warmed serving platter.
- Reduce sauce over medium heat, adjusting seasoning. Pour sauce over mussels and garnish with parsley.

FIORI DI ZUCCHINI FRITTI
Deep-Fried Stuffed Zucchini Flowers

12 zucchini flowers*
8 oz. (225 g) very firm
  Ricotta cheese
2 oz. (60 g) Gorgonzola
  cheese
2 oz. (60 g) Parmesan
  cheese, grated
1 egg yolk
Salt and freshly
  ground black pepper
Corn oil
3 tbsp. (45 mL) flour
1 pinch baking powder
6 tbsp. (90 mL) dry
  white wine
1 piled tbsp. (15 mL)
  fresh mint, minced
2 lemons
Parsley sprigs

* Zucchini flowers may be found during summer and early fall in Italian green-grocers and farmers' markets. Also ask for them from friends who grow the prolific zucchini in their backyards.

- Brush zucchini flowers and remove and discard pistils from inside. Thoroughly mix together cheeses and egg yolk, seasoning to taste.
- Spoon cheese mixture into a piping bag and pipe some into each flower to 1/4" (0.5 cm) of top. Fold in tips of petals to close. If possible, refrigerate for 4-6 hours.
- Heat 1"-2" (2.5-5 cm) oil in heavy saucepan to 340°F (170°C).
- Combine flour, baking powder and enough wine to make a soup-like batter. Stir in mint.
- Dip flowers in turn in batter to coat them, shake off excess batter and deep fry in preheated oil until golden brown.
- Arrange 3 fried flowers on folded paper towels on each serving plate. Garnish with wedges of lemon and sprigs of parsley.

INSALATE

INSALATA DI TONNO CON FAGIOLE E POMODORO
Fresh Tuna, Bean and Tomato Salad

1 cup (235 g) cooked
white beans
(Cannellini or
Romano), drained
Juice of 1 lemon
2 tsp. (10 mL) fresh
marjoram
1 clove garlic, crushed
6 tbsp. (90 mL) olive oil
Salt and freshly
ground black pepper
1 lb. (455 g) slice of
fresh tuna, about 1/2"
(1.25 cm) thick
2 medium vine
tomatoes, peeled,
cored, and cut in
wedges
4 large lettuce leaves

- Marinate beans in half the lemon juice, 1 tsp. (5 mL) marjoram, crushed garlic, 4 tbsp. (60 mL) olive oil and salt and pepper to taste for 3 hours in refrigerator.
- Remove beans from refrigerator, discarding garlic, and allow them to reach room temperature.
- Sauté tuna in a little olive oil, 90 seconds each side. Allow to cool, then dice.
- Gently combine beans, tomato and tuna. Dress with remaining oil and lemon juice and adjust seasoning.
- To serve, spoon into lettuce leaves and garnish with rest of marjoram.

INSALATA D'ENDIVA BELGA, PROSCIUTTO E PARMIGIANO
Belgian Endive (Chicory) Salad with Prosciutto and Parmesan

3 egg yolks
2 tsp. (10 mL) Dijon
   mustard
1/2 cup (120 mL) light
   olive oil
5 shallots, minced
2 tbsp. (30 mL) parsley,
   chopped
2 tbsp. (30 mL) fresh
   lemon juice
Salt and freshly
   ground black pepper
2 heads Belgian endive
   (chicory)
8 large, very thin slices
   of prosciutto
4 tbsp. (60 mL)
   Parmesan cheese,
   thinly shaved

- Blend egg yolks and mustard in a blender or food processor. With machine still running, very slowly pour in oil. The dressing will thicken. Pour into a bowl, add shallot, parsley and lemon juice and mix well. Season to taste.
- Trim bottom off endive. Pull off individual leaves. On 4 serving plates, arrange leaves in two rows, with tips facing outwards.
- Place slices of prosciutto between rows of leaves. Spoon a little dressing into the hollow of each leaf, garnish with shaved Parmesan and serve.

INSALATA GENARO
Tomato and Arugula Salad with Roast Garlic Dressing

3 medium heads of garlic, peeled
6 small anchovy filets, drained
2 tbsp. (30 mL) white wine vinegar
1 cup (235 mL) olive oil
Salt and freshly ground black pepper
1 bunch arugula (Italian salad greens)
4 vine tomatoes, peeled, cored and thinly sliced

- Roast peeled garlic cloves on an oiled tray at 375°F (190°C) until nutty brown and soft. Remove and allow to cool.
- Put garlic and anchovy in blender or food processor. Blend into a paste and, with machine running, slowly add vinegar first, then oil. Season to taste.
- Trim and wash arugula and shake dry. Tear into pieces and lay a bed of leaves on each serving plate. Arrange a a fan of tomato slices on each bed of arugula, spoon some dressing on tomato and garnish with an extra grind of black pepper.

Arugula

ZUPPE

MINESTRA PEPERONI FREDDO
Chilled Roast Pepper Soup

5 red bell peppers
2 cups (475 mL) canned
  plum tomatoes,
  drained and sieved
2 medium cloves garlic,
  minced
3 tbsp. (45 mL) olive oil
3 cups (710 mL) chicken
  stock
Salt and freshly
  ground black pepper
Basil leaves, cut in fine
  strips

- Roast peppers over gas flame or under broiler until outer skin is black. Seal in a plastic bag and allow to sweat for 10 minutes. Peel peppers under cold running water without breaking flesh. Cut open and remove core and seeds.
- Purée 3/4 of peppers and all tomatoes together. Gently sauté garlic in olive oil until nutty brown, add pepper-tomato purée and chicken stock.
- Bring soup to boil and simmer gently for 10-12 minutes, seasoning to taste.
- Allow soup to cool. Refrigerate in covered container.
- Serve in chilled bowls, garnished with basil and rest of red pepper, julienned.

ZUPPA DI PESCE CAPRESE
Capri Seafood Soup

1/2 lb. (225 g) white fish bones
2 tsp. (10 mL) sea salt
3 tbsp. (45 mL) olive oil
1 medium onion, diced
2 stalks celery, with outside trimmed, diced
1 clove garlic, minced
2 plum tomatoes, peeled and chopped coarsely
1 tsp. (5 mL) grated lemon zest
Salt and freshly ground black pepper
1/2 lb. (225 g) mussels
4 raw shrimp, shelled and deveined
1/2 lb. (225 g) fish (halibut, sole, tuna or salmon) in 1/2" (1.25 cm) dice
1/2 cup (120 mL) dry white wine
1 tsp. (5 mL) fresh marjoram (or fresh oregano and thyme)

- To make fish stock, cover fish bones with cold water, add sea salt, bring to boil and simmer for 15 minutes.
- Meanwhile gently sauté onion, celery and garlic in olive oil for 5 minutes. Add tomatoes, lemon zest and pepper to taste and continue cooking until onion and celery are tender.
- Raise heat, add mussels, shrimp and fish. Sauté for 30 seconds, then add wine and cook for another minute.
- Add strained fish stock, simmer for 2 minutes, seasoning to taste. Ladle into warmed soup bowls, including mussel shells, and serve garnished with fresh herbs.

PIZZA E PASTA

PIZZA DOUGH

1 cup (235 mL) warm
water
1 package active dry
yeast
3-1/2 cups (830 mL)
flour
1/2 tsp. (2 mL) salt
1 tbsp. (15 mL) olive oil

For 6 small pizzas

- Mix warm water and yeast in a large bowl. Add half the flour, mixed with salt, and stir until completely mixed.
- Add olive oil and work in rest of the flour by hand to form a dough. Kneading should take 5-10 minutes.
- Dough is ready when it no longer sticks to hands. Form into a ball, coat with a little more olive oil and put in a large covered bowl to warm. In a gas oven, the pilot light will provide enough heat; in an electric oven, preheat to 200°F (95°C) then turn off. Let dough rise for 45 minutes.
- Punch dough down and divide into six equal parts, each will be enough for one 8" (20 cm) pizza. Roll out each piece on a well-floured surface to 1/8" (0.3 cm) thickness. Cut to 9" (23 cm) diameter, fold in 3/8" (1 cm) of outside edge and crimp.
- Dough is now ready for topping. It should be cooked

in a preheated oven at 550-
600°F (285-315°C). If some
bricks or unglazed tiles are
available, they should be
laid on baking sheet with
pizza placed directly on top.
Left-over dough, wrapped
in plastic, may be kept in
refrigerator for later use.

PIZZETTA AL SARDINAIRA

Dough for 8" (20 cm)
  pizza (see page 84)
1 tbsp. (15 mL) olive oil
1 clove garlic, crushed
1 pinch dried
  marjoram
Salt and freshly
  ground black pepper
1 large tomato, cored,
  peeled, chopped and
  squeezed dry
1/4 medium red onion,
  very thinly sliced
12 fresh sardine filets,
  skinned and julienned
1 tsp. (5 mL) capers,
  drained

- Brush pizza base with oil
  and scatter with crushed
  garlic. Sprinkle with
  marjoram, black pepper and
  very little salt.
- Spread tomato and onion
  evenly over base, then
  arrange sardine filets in a
  grid pattern on top and
  sprinkle on capers.
- Bake in very hot oven, 550-
  600°F (285-315°C) for 8-10
  minutes, when crust should
  be golden brown.

Serves one person

PIZZETTA GIOVANNI

10 cloves garlic, peeled
Dough for 8" (20 cm)
  pizza (see page 84)
1 tbsp. (15 mL) olive oil
1 pinch dried oregano
Freshly ground black
  pepper
3 oz. (85 g) soft goat
  cheese rolled into 6
  small sausage
  shapes, each 3" (7.5
  cm) long
3 tbsp. (45 mL) tomato,
  peeled, cored and
  coarsely chopped

Serves one person

- Roast garlic cloves on oiled baking sheet in medium hot oven until soft.
- Brush rolled out pizza base with oil and sprinkle with oregano and pepper to taste.
- Arrange cheese in six spokes radiating from centre of pizza base to crimped edge. Spread some of tomato and garlic cloves between cheese spokes.
- Bake in very hot oven, 550-600°F (285-315°C) for 8-10 minutes, when crust should be golden brown.

FUSILLI CON RAPINI, FUNGHI E POMODORI
Spiral Pasta with Rapini, Wild Mushrooms and Tomatoes

3 tbsp. (45 mL) olive oil
4 cloves garlic,
  chopped
5 shallots, peeled and
  chopped

- Heat oil in a large shallow sauté pan. Sauté garlic, shallot and liberal grinding of black pepper until garlic is nutty brown. Take porcini

Black pepper, freshly
  ground
1/2 oz. (15 g) dried
  porcini, rinsed and
  soaked in 1/2 cup (120
  mL) warm water for
  at least 30 minutes.
4 oz. (115 g) fresh
  oyster mushrooms
8 oz. (225 g) rapini
  (Italian greens),
  washed, trimmed
  and torn up
1/4 cup (60 mL) dry
  white wine
2 medium plum
  tomatoes, peeled and
  coarsely chopped
1 lb. (455 g) fusilli
  (spiral-shaped pasta)
  Salt and freshly
  ground black pepper
2 tbsp. (30 mL) sweet
  butter
6 oz. (170 g) Parmesan
  cheese, coarsely
  grated

from water, but keep water.
Squeeze porcini dry in paper
towel and wipe oyster
mushrooms with towel.
Coarsely chop both kinds of
mushrooms.

- Add mushrooms to pan and
  sauté for 1 minute, then add
  rapini and sauté 1 minute
  more. Mix in wine, tomato
  and 2 tbsp. (30 mL)
  mushroom soaking water,
  bring to boil and remove
  from heat.

- Meanwhile have pasta
  cooking in plenty of boiling
  salted water. When cooked
  al dente, drain thoroughly.
  Adjust seasoning of sauce
  and mix in pasta.

- As sauce is being tossed
  through pasta, add butter
  and cheese. Serve
  immediately in warmed
  bowls.

FARFALLINE ROMANTICHE
Butterfly Pasta with Prosciutto and Asparagus

1 lb. (455 g) asparagus, cut into 1" (2.5 cm) pieces
Juice of 1 lemon
Salt and freshly ground black pepper
1 1/2 cups (355 mL) whipping cream
4 oz. (115 g) prosciutto, finely julienned
1 lb. (455 g) farfalline (small butterfly-shaped pasta)
6 oz. (170 g) Parmesan cheese, coarsely grated
2 tbsp. (30 mL) sweet butter, softened
1/2 oz. (15 g) Parmesan cheese, shaved and julienned

- Put cut asparagus in large saucepan with lemon juice, seasoning and just enough water to cover. Bring to boil and simmer until water has almost evaporated. Add cream and prosciutto, return to boil and simmer for 1 minute, then remove from heat.
- Meanwhile have pasta cooking in plenty of boiling salted water. When cooked al dente, drain well.
- Adjust seasoning of sauce, pour pasta on sauce and while tossing into sauce, add grated cheese and butter.
- Serve immediately in warmed bowls, garnished with julienned Parmesan.

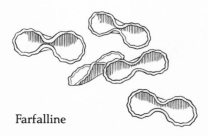

Farfalline

PESCE

SALMONE CON PORRI E ZAFFERANO
Salmon with Leeks and Saffron

3 tbsp. (45 mL) sweet
butter, softened
4 filets of Atlantic
salmon, about 7 oz.
(200 g) each
2 tbsp. (30 mL) flour
Salt and freshly
ground black pepper
1 leek
1/2 cup (120 mL) dry
white wine
3/4 cup (175 mL) fish
stock (see recipe for
Capri Seafood Soup,
page 83)
1 pinch saffron

- Heat 2 tbsp. (30 mL) butter in pan large enough to hold all four filets. Season filets and dust lightly with flour. Seal filets on both sides and remove from pan.
- Rinse leek, discard green leaves, halve and julienne. Add remaining butter to same pan and sauté leek until tender. Add white wine, bring to boil, then add fish stock and saffron and return to boil.
- Put filets in stock and simmer gently for 5 minutes.
- When fish is cooked, remove to warmed serving plates. Reduce stock over high heat until it begins to thicken, adjust seasoning and spoon over filets. Serve with appropriate fresh vegetables.

CALAMARI RIPIENI CON FUNGHI
Braised Squid Stuffed with Wild Mushrooms

12 medium whole
   squid
1 oz. (30 g) dried
   porcini
1 cup (235 mL) fresh
   mushrooms, sliced
1 tbsp. (15 mL) garlic,
   minced
1/2 small onion,
   chopped
1/2 cup (120 mL) olive
   oil
1 tbsp. (15 mL) parsley,
   chopped
1/3 cup (80 mL)
   breadcrumbs
Salt and freshly
   ground black pepper
1/2 cup (120 mL) dry
   white wine
Parsley sprigs

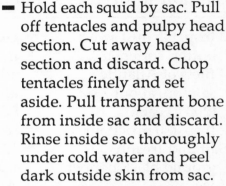

Squid

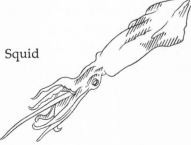

- Hold each squid by sac. Pull off tentacles and pulpy head section. Cut away head section and discard. Chop tentacles finely and set aside. Pull transparent bone from inside sac and discard. Rinse inside sac thoroughly under cold water and peel dark outside skin from sac.
- Meanwhile soak dried mushrooms in 2 cups (475 mL) warm water for least 30 minutes. Drain off and keep soaking liquid. Rinse reconstituted mushrooms well and pat dry.
- In a heavy skillet, sauté garlic and onion in 1/4 cup (60 mL) olive oil until golden. Add fresh mushroom slices and sauté until almost dry. Then add reconstituted wild mushrooms and soaking liquid and cook until most of liquid has evaporated. Set aside and allow to cool.
- Combine cooled mushroom

mixture, chopped tentacles, parsley, breadcrumbs, 1 tsp. (5 mL) salt and generous grinding of black pepper in a food processor and blend until completely amalgamated.

- Set aside at least 1 tbsp. (15 mL) of stuffing for sauce. Spoon remainder into sacs, leaving enough room in each to seal opening with a toothpick. Any stuffing left over can also be used to enrich sauce.
- Take a sauté pan large enough to hold stuffed sacs in one layer. With remaining oil, sauté stuffed sacs until well browned. Add white wine and remaining stuffing to oil and adjust seasoning. Cover and simmer over low heat for 20-30 minutes. Squid will be cooked when a toothpick pierces sacs easily.
- Divide squid on four serving plates. If sauce is too thick, add a little water; if too thin, quickly reduce over high heat. Adjust seasoning. Pour sauce over squid and serve garnished with parsley.

TONNA ALLA SICILIANA
Sautéed Tuna with Sicilian Vegetables

6 tbsp. (90 mL) olive oil
1 medium potato,
  cooked in skin for 10
  minutes, peeled and
  diced
1 red bell pepper, cored
  and finely diced
1/2 onion, finely diced
Salt and freshly
  ground black pepper
4 tuna steaks, 1/2" (1.5
  cm) thick, about 7 oz.
  (200 g) each
1 tbsp. (15 mL) capers,
  drained
2 tbsp. (30 mL) chopped
  parsley
1/4 cup (60 mL)
  balsamic vinegar

- In 4 tbsp. (60 mL) olive oil, sauté diced potato, bell pepper and onion gently for 10 minutes, seasoning to taste.
- In a heavy skillet, heat remaining oil and sauté seasoned tuna steaks for 2 minutes on each side. Remove and set on warmed serving plates.
- Raise heat under sautéed vegetables, adding capers, parsley and vinegar. Reduce for 3 minutes, then spoon over tuna steaks and serve.

PESCE ALLA VENEZIANA
Venetian Fish

4 eggs
1 pinch salt
1/4 cup (60 mL) milk
2 lb. (1 kg) pickerel
   filets
1/2 cup (120 mL) olive
   oil
4 tbsp. (60 mL) sweet
   butter
2 medium onions,
   thinly sliced
2 cloves garlic, minced
1/2 cup (120 mL) white
   wine vinegar
1 bay leaf
1 cup (235 mL) water
Salt and freshly
   ground black pepper
2 cups (475 mL)
   vegetable oil
1 cup (235 mL) fine
   breadcrumbs
4 heaped tbsp. (60 mL)
   raisins, presoaked in
   warm water
2 tbsp. (30 mL) pine
   nuts, toasted
2 tbsp. (30 mL) parsley,
   chopped

- Beat together eggs and milk with pinch of salt. Cut pickerel into pieces 2" by 4" (5 cm by 10 cm) and leave to marinate in egg mixture for 1 hour.
- Heat oil and butter and sauté onion and garlic until they look translucent. Add vinegar and bay leaf and simmer for 1 minute. Add water, season to taste and simmer gently for 30 minutes. Set aside.
- In heavy saucepan heat vegetable oil to 375°F (190°C). Remove fish pieces from marinade, shaking off excess. Coat each piece uniformly on all sides in breadcrumbs. Fry pieces until golden brown. Pat pieces dry and keep warm.
- Reheat sauce, removing bay leaf and blending in raisins, pine nuts and parsley. Arrange fish slices on serving plates and garnish with sauce.

ANIMELLE CON SCALOGNE ARRISTE E SALSA DI MADEIRA
Sweetbreads with Roast Shallots and Madeira Sauce

1 small onion, chopped
1 bay leaf
1 clove
1 tbsp. (15 mL) coarse salt
1-1/4 lbs. (565 g) fresh sweetbreads
24 whole shallots, peeled
1 tbsp. (15 mL) olive oil
4 tbsp. (60 mL) flour
3 tbsp. (45 mL) sweet butter, softened
3/4 cup (175 mL) Madeira
2 tbsp. (30 mL) parsley, chopped
Salt and freshly ground black pepper

- Boil 10 cups (2.50 L) of water, add onion, bay leaf, clove and salt and simmer for 5 minutes. Rinse sweetbreads, add to stock and simmer gently for 2 minutes. Cool in stock at room temperature for 1 hour.
- When sweetbreads have cooled, carefully remove outer membranes and any fat or arteries by hand and return cleaned sweetbreads to stock. Store in covered container in refrigerator.
- On oiled tray, bake shallots at medium heat until soft.
- Take sweetbreads from stock, pat dry and cut into slices 1/2" (1.25 cm) thick. Dust slices with flour and sauté both sides in 1 tbsp. (15 mL) butter. Add shallots and Madeira and cook for 2 minutes. If sauce is too dry, add some stock.

- Arrange sweetbread slices on warmed serving plates. Reduce sauce slightly, adding parsley and seasoning to taste. Blend in remaining butter to enrich and pour over sweetbreads. Serve with vegetables of choice.

SCALOPPINE DI VITELLO
Veal Scallopine with Fennel and Cream

1/2 bulb fresh fennel
1 lb. (455 g) Provimi veal, cut into 16 slices, beaten thin with flat side of cleaver
Salt and freshly ground black pepper
Flour
3 tbsp. (45 mL) sweet butter, softened
1/2 cup (120 mL) dry white wine
1 cup (235 mL) whipping cream
3 tbsp. (45 mL) fresh green fennel leaf, chopped

- Steam fennel over boiling water. When tender, allow to cool and cut into 1/4" (0.5 cm) pieces.
- Season and lightly flour veal scallopine. Heat 1 tbsp. (15 mL) butter in heavy skillet and sauté scallopine 10 seconds each side and keep warm on serving plates.
- Heat remaining butter in skillet, sauté fennel for 1 minute, add wine and loosen meat glaze. Add cream, season to taste and reduce until sauce begins to thicken.
- Spoon sauce over scallopine. Garnish with fennel green and serve with chosen side vegetables.

LONZA DI MAIALE ARROSTO CON FICHI, CIPOLLE, PIGNOLE E MARSALA
Roast Pork Tenderloin with Figs, Scallions, Pine Nuts and Marsala

1 cup (235 mL) Marsala
10 dried figs in 1/8" (0.3 cm) slices
4 filets pork tenderloin, each about 7 oz. (200 g)
Salt and freshly ground black pepper
3 tbsp. (45 mL) olive oil
1 clove garlic, minced
4 tbsp. (60 mL) scallions or green onions, finely chopped
2 tbsp. (30 mL) pine nuts, toasted
2 tbsp. (30 mL) sweet butter, softened
1 tbsp. (15 mL) parsley, chopped

- Soak sliced figs in marsala overnight.
- Remove sinew from outside of tenderloin pieces and season them. Warm olive oil over high heat in sauté pan. Seal meat and set aside. Reduce heat and sauté garlic until it begins to brown. Add scallions, pine nuts, figs and Marsala. Bring to boil, reduce heat and return meat to sauce. In preheated 375°F (190°C) oven, bake meat and sauce for 8 minutes, adding a little water if it seems too dry.
- Remove tenderloin filets from sauce and allow to rest for 2 minutes. Carve filets diagonally in 1/8" (0.3 cm) slices and keep warm.
- Pour any juice from meat into sauce, return to simmer, adjust seasoning and blend in butter.

LONZA DI MAIALE ARROSTO CON FICHI, CIPOLLE, PIGNOLE E MARSALA
Roast Pork Tenderloin with Figs, Scallions, Pine Nuts and Marsala

ORSO – PAGE 96

IL DIPLOMATICO
Rum and Coffee Flavored
Chocolate Layer Cake
ORSO – PAGE 99

MINESTRA DI GRANO
Corn Chowder
PRONTO – PAGE 110

- Spoon sauce onto warmed serving plates, fan pork slices over sauce and garnish with parsley. Serve with side vegetables of choice.

POLLO ALLA CARCIOFI E ZINZERO
Braised Chicken with Artichokes and Ginger

1-1/2 oz. (45 g) unpeeled fresh ginger

8 large marinated artichoke hearts

4 tbsp. (60 mL) olive oil

2 free-range chickens, about 2 lbs. (905 g) each, cut in half and boned

Salt and freshly ground black pepper

2 cloves garlic, minced

5 black peppercorns, coarsely crushed

1/2 cup (120 mL) dry white wine

1/2 cup (120 mL) chicken stock

- Cook ginger in water for 45 minutes. Let cool, peel and cut into julienne slices. Drain and pat dry artichoke hearts and divide into sixths.
- In heavy skillet large enough to hold 4 chicken halves, heat 2 tbsp. (30 mL) olive oil. Season chicken and sauté until golden brown both sides. Set aside and keep warm.
- Add remaining oil to same skillet and sauté garlic, julienned ginger and cracked peppercorns until garlic begins to brown. Add

2 tbsp. (30 mL) sweet
butter, softened
1 tbsp. (15 mL) fresh
mint, chopped

artichoke and sauté 1 minute more.

- Return chicken halves, skin side up, to skillet, pour in wine and reduce by half over medium heat. Then add chicken stock and simmer gently for 15 minutes, adding more stock if needed.
- Again remove chicken and keep warm. Bring sauce to fast boil, adjusting seasoning and blending in butter. Then remove from heat.
- Spoon sauce onto warmed serving plates, arrange chicken on sauce and garnish with mint. Serve with side vegetable of choice.

$$\boxed{\text{D O L C E}}$$

IL DIPLOMATICO
Rum and Coffee Flavored
Chocolate Layer Cake

---

12 oz. (340 g) semi-
  sweet chocolate
1-1/2 cups (355 mL)
  strong hot coffee
2 tbsp. (30 mL) freeze-
  dried coffee
1/4 cup (60 mL) dark
  rum
1-1/2 tbsp. (20 mL)
  sugar
1 lb. (455 g) pound
  cake, cut in 1/4" (0.5
  cm) slices
5 egg yolks
1 tsp. (5 mL) dark cocoa
  powder
5 egg whites
1/2 cup (120 mL)
  whipping cream,
  beaten stiff

- Break up 5 oz. (140 g) chocolate into a metal baking pan and melt in a 225°F (105°C) oven.
- Line a 9" by 4" (23 cm by 10 cm) loaf pan with wax paper.
- Mix 1 tbsp. (15 mL) sugar, the freeze-dried coffee and the rum into the hot coffee and allow to cool.
- Line bottom and sides of loaf pan with cake slices, but leave enough slices for a middle and top layer.
- Spoon enough coffee mixture into pan to soak lining of cake slices.
- Whisk egg yolks and remaining sugar in double-boiler until mixture looks pale yellow. Add cocoa powder and mix until dissolved.
- Pour yolk mixture into bowl and combine with molten chocolate. Beat egg whites until stiff. First mix 1 tbsp.

(15 mL) egg white into chocolate mixture, then carefully fold in remaining egg white.

- Fill half lined pan with egg-chocolate mixture. Lay down a middle layer of sliced cake, soaked in coffee-rum mixture. Spoon in remaining egg-chocolate filling and top with a final layer of soaked cake.
- Seal pan with plastic wrap and refrigerate overnight.
- Next day, melt remaining chocolate. Turn chilled cake from pan onto a cooling rack. Remove wax paper and coat entire surface with a thin layer of melted chocolate. Return to refrigerator to harden chocolate.
- Place on serving platter, garnish with whipped cream and serve in slices.

TORTA AL MARSALA CON FRAGOLE
Marsala Tart with Strawberries

1 cup (235 mL) sugar
9 tbsp. (130 mL) sweet
 butter, softened
3/4 cup (170 g) flour
6-1/2 oz. (190 mL)
 Marsala
5 egg yolks
1 lb. (455 g)
 strawberries,
 washed, hulled and
 dried
1-1/2 cups (355 mL)
 whipping cream,
 beaten stiff

- Blend 4 tbsp. (60 mL) sugar and 8 tbsp. (115 mL) butter. Into this work flour and 2 tbsp. (30 mL) Marsala to form a soft dough.
- Butter and lightly flour a 12" (30 cm) tart pan. Roll out dough thinly and line pan. Bake in preheated 380°F (195°C) oven until pastry is crisp and golden brown, about 4 minutes.
- Whisk egg yolks with remaining sugar and Marsala over a double boiler until it becomes thick and creamy. Allow to cool slightly, then pour into baked tart shell.
- Arrange strawberries, pressed down slightly into egg mixture, in concentric rings.
- Let rest for 1 hour at room temperature. Serve cut into wedges, with whipped cream on the side.

Orso Recommended   Wines

BIANCHI:
Orvieto Classico
  Vigneto La Fontana (Villa Fratina 1984)**
Arneis del Roero (Malvira 1984)*
Chardonnay (Instituto di San Michele 1984)**

ROSSI:
Dolcetto D'Alba Nassone (Elvia Cogno 1984)**
Cabernet Sauvignon di Miralduolo (Lungarotti 1979)*
Barolo Brunate (Marcarini 1980)**

* Liquor Control Board of Ontario Vintages stock
** Private import

Pronto

Mark McEwen

*T*he name Pronto says it, the smart blue-tiled facade on Mount Pleasant Road underlines it: it is the simple statement of the word "pronto", which in Italian means ready or prompt or on the telephone, as you may know if you've seen many Italian movies, hello.

Once inside you observe the point of the name and the statement. There always seem to be many waiters on the move and, at the back, in the very visible open kitchen, many vibrant young sous-chefs, in impeccable white hats and uniforms, busily at work.

But so fashionably popular has the restaurant become that at times the meaning "prompt" takes, despite every effort by its staff, an ironic undertone. At those times, it seems that everyone hungry in the city wants a seat in one of Pronto's pink chairs or banquettes in order to relish its renowned Northern Italian food.

Pronto, following in the successful footsteps of its competitor Biffi, across the street, did begin by Northern Italian inspiration. But of its three present co-owners, the one who inspires and guides its cuisine is in fact a young expatriate American who arrived in Canada with the lowliest of catering experiences, if with considerable ambitions in the kitchen.

Mark McEwan is a slim, quiet and, at first encounter, an almost retiring man. He scarcely seems to reflect the smart urgency implied by his restaurant's name and yet from the moment of joining it in 1985 he has been paramount in confirming its reputation for fine and highly inventive cuisine.

His ascent in the hierarchy of respected Toronto chefs has been swift and remarkable. While he did study at George Brown College, which supplies the city's catering industry with much of its trained staff, he claims that like all authentic chefs he trained himself. And he does give the impression of being a young man still searching for the ultimate fulfilment of his profession.

His rapid attainment of executive chef's role in the Sutton Place Hotel might have been regarded by anyone else as professional fulfilment. But having reached that peak and found it insufficient, Mark McEwan cut loose and joined two non-culinary partners in running Pronto.

By comparison with the other chefs noted in this book, he joined the friendly battle for eminence in new Italian cuisine rather late. But he is quite blunt in asserting that his interest is in fine cooking rather than in authentic Northern Italian cooking. It just happens that the current style of Italian cooking suits his present inventive purposes. And he is a notably inventive chef, never entirely happy with his menu, never entirely satisfied that any of the dishes on it cannot be improved upon.

He does seem satisfied, however, to have settled in Toronto, and is content that here he can reach for anything his ambitions require at the moment. His objectives are clear enough: the very best of ingredients, which he seeks out and buys himself, cooked in the most straightforward and striking way. That what he produces is delectably good satisfies him for the moment; that it is authentically Italian is not so important. That it satisfies and delights his clients and admirers is some reward, but undoubtedly what draws him on, and will continue to do so, is pursuit of the very best.

For that pursuit Mark McEwan and his staff at Pronto are very obviously at the ready.

PRONTO RISTORANTE, 692 Mount Pleasant Road.
Telephone: 486-1111. Open Monday to Saturday: for lunch 11.30 a.m. to 3 p.m.; for dinner 5 p.m. to 1 a.m. Closed Sundays and statutory holidays. Fully licensed. Major cards accepted.
Reservations recommended.

| ANTIPASTI |

ZUCCHINI AL TIMO
Zucchini with Thyme

4 medium zucchini
1 tbsp. (15 mL) sweet
  butter
2 tsp. (10 mL) shallots
  or onions, chopped
2 cloves garlic, minced
Salt and freshly
  ground black pepper
  and nutmeg
1/4 cup (60 mL) dry
  white wine
2 cups (475 mL)
  whipping cream
1 small tomato, cored
  and coarsely chopped
2 tbsp. (30 mL) sun-
  dried tomatoes,
  julienned
2 tsp. (10 mL) fresh
  thyme leaves or 1 tsp.
  (5 mL) dried thyme
4 tbsp. (60 mL) goat
  cheese, crumbled

- Cut zucchini in halves, scoop seeds from each half and cut into long julienne slices like fettucini.
- Heat butter in a skillet, sauté shallot until soft, then add garlic and seasoning to taste. Continue cooking for a minute, then stir in wine. Add cream and cook over high heat to reduce slightly. Add fresh and sun-dried tomatoes, thyme and cheese and whisk until sauce is smooth. Keep warm.
- In boiling salted water, blanch sliced zucchini for 10 seconds. Drain and dress with sauce before serving.

COZZE CON CREMA E BASILICA
Mussels with Fresh Basil Cream

4 tbsp. (60 mL) sweet
butter
4 tbsp. (60 mL) onion,
finely chopped
2 cloves garlic, crushed
1/2 tsp. (2 mL) white
peppercorns, coarsely
crushed
2 bay leaves
Salt
4 lbs. (1.80 kg) cultured
mussels (from Prince
Edward Island, if
available)
1/2 cup (120 mL) dry
white wine

- Sauté onion in butter in a large heavy saucepan until it turns translucent, add garlic, crushed pepper, bay leaves and salt to taste and sauté for one minute more.
- Meanwhile scrub and beard mussels, discarding any that are not closed. Add wine and 2 cups (475 mL) water to saucepan, then mussels and bring to boil. Cover saucepan and cook over high heat until all mussels are open, about 3 minutes.
- Remove mussels, discard empty top shell of each. Put other shells containing mussels on serving dish to keep warm. Strain remaining juices through cheesecloth and set aside for sauce (see next page).

Salsa basilica fresca
Fresh Basil Cream

2 tbsp. (30 mL) sweet
  butter
1/2 white portion of a
  leek, finely julienned
1-1/2 tsp. (7 mL) garlic,
  minced
6 tbsp. (90 mL) tomato
  concasse (crushed
  fresh pulp of skinned
  and seeded tomato)
2 pinches each of white
  pepper, salt and
  nutmeg
Juice of 1 lemon
1-1/2 cups (355 mL)
  approximately of
  mussel cooking liquid
1 cup (235 mL)
  whipping cream
4 tbsp. (60 mL) fresh
  basil, finely chopped
  at last moment

- Heat butter in sauté pan until it foams. Add leek, garlic, tomato, seasoned with pepper, salt and nutmeg, sauté for 3 minutes, then add lemon juice and mussel liquid and reduce by one third over medium heat.
- Add cream and again reduce by one third, adjusting seasoning.
- Add chopped basil, bring quickly to boil and at once pour generously and evenly over warm mussels. Must be served at once or basil tint will fade.

$$\boxed{\text{Z U P P E}}$$

BISQUE DI CIPOLLE
Red Onion Bisque

4 tbsp. (60 mL) sweet
  butter
2 medium red onions,
  thinly sliced
2 tbsp. (30 mL) dry
  white wine
Salt, freshly ground
  white pepper and
  nutmeg
2 cups (475 mL) chicken
  stock
2 cups (475 mL)
  whipping cream
1/4 cup (60 mL) smoked
  salmon, julienned
Parsley or chives,
  chopped

— In half the butter, sauté onion over medium heat until it is translucent. Add white wine and season to taste with salt, pepper and nutmeg. Simmer until wine has fully evaporated, then add chicken stock and cook until reduced by half. Add cream and again cook until reduced by half. Stir in and incorporate rest of butter.
— Divide julienned salmon into four serving bowls. Pour some boiling soup into each and serve garnished with parsley or chives.

MINESTRA DI GRANO
Corn Chowder

2/3 tbsp. (10 mL) sweet
  butter
2 tbsp. (30 mL) onion,
  diced
3 tbsp. (45 mL) celery
  stalk, diced

— Melt butter in heavy saucepan and sauté onion, celery and cucumber without browning until soft. Stir in flour until fully incorporated, then season to taste with

3 tbsp. (45 mL)
cucumber, peeled,
seeded and diced

1-1/2 tbsp. (20 mL)
flour

Salt and freshly
ground white pepper
and nutmeg

3 cups (710 mL) chicken
stock

1-1/3 cups (315 mL)
whipping cream

10 oz. (285 g) frozen
corn kernels

1 tbsp. (15 mL) fresh
dill, finely chopped

2 oz. (60 mL) puff
pastry

1 egg, well beaten

salt, pepper and nutmeg. Stir in stock slowly, fully blending it. Bring to boil and simmer covered for an hour.

- Add corn to soup and simmer for about 10 minutes until soft. Meanwhile cook cream in another sauté pan until reduced by half.

- Pour soup into a blender or food processor and process until creamy smooth. Strain back into saucepan and bring to the boil, then stir in cream and chopped dill.

- Pour soup into four cold narrow-mouthed soup cups or bowls. Roll out pastry and cut into rounds to fit over cups. Damp rims of cups and cover with pastry. Brush pastry with egg wash and bake in preheated 400°F (205°C) oven for 10 minutes or until pastry is golden brown. Serve very hot.

INSALATE

CAROTE VINAIGRETTE
Carrot Vinaigrette

6 tbsp. (90 mL) fresh
  carrot juice
6 tbsp. (90 mL) light
  vegetable oil
3 tbsp. (45 mL) red
  wine vinegar
1 tbsp. (15 mL) fresh
  lemon juice
Salt and freshly
  ground white pepper
1 tsp. (5 mL) fresh dill,
  minced
4 servings of radicchio,
  Belgian endive, curly
  endive, arugula, or
  Boston heart lettuce.
  Or mixture of these.

- Process all liquid ingredients
  for 30 seconds. Season to
  taste, then stir in dill.
- Arrange salad greens on
  plates and splash with
  dressing just before serving.

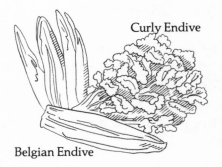

Curly Endive

Belgian Endive

INSALATA DI CACIOTTA DI CAPRA CALDO
Warm Goat's Cheese Salad

2 discs of firm goat
  cheese, 3-1/2 oz.
  (100 g) each, cut in
  half horizontally
Assorted salad greens
  (as available):

- Bake disc of cheese under
  broiler until soft and golden
  brown.
- Meanwhile arrange salad
  greens on 4 serving plates as
  naturally and decoratively

radicchio, curly white
or Belgian endive,
oakleaf or butter
lettuce, or arugula
4 pieces preserved sun-
dried tomato, finely
julienned
2 tsp. (10 g) pine nuts
Salt and freshly
ground white pepper

as possible. Sprinkle each
with julienned tomato and
pine nuts.
- Place baked cheese at centre
of each plate. Sprinkle
vinaigrette (see page 114),
warmed but not boiled, over
both cheese and salad
greens.
- Season further if desired.

CACIOTTA DI CAPRA AL PEPE
Goat Cheese with Peppercorns

1 tsp. (5 mL) shallot,
finely chopped
1/4 tsp. (1.2 mL) Dijon
mustard
1/2 tsp. (2 mL) fresh
lemon juice
1 tbsp. (15 mL)
raspberry vinegar
4 tbsp. (60 mL) light
vegetable oil
Salt and freshly
ground white pepper
4 discs firm Canadian
goat cheese, 2 oz.
(60 g) each

(cont...)

- In a closed container, shake
together shallot, mustard,
lemon juice, vinegar and oil,
with seasoning to taste,
until well mixed.
- Set cheese discs at centre of
four serving plates and
garnish generously with
crushed peppercorns and
chives. Decorate rim of each
plate with coarsely-
shredded lettuce leaves.
- Drizzle dressing over both
cheese and lettuce and
serve.

4 tsp. (20 mL) chives,
   finely chopped
2 tsp. (10 mL) white
   peppercorns, coarsely
   crushed
16 arugula leaves (or
   suitable salad greens)
8 radicchio leaves

VINAIGRETTE

2 tbsp. (30 mL) vintage
   red wine vinegar
1/2 cup (120 mL)
   peanut oil
1/4 cup (60 mL) virgin
   olive oil
1/2 tbsp. (7 mL) Dijon
   mustard
4 fresh basil leaves,
   minced
Pinch garlic, minced
1 tsp. (5 mL) shallot,
   minced
1 tsp. (5 mL) fresh
   lemon juice
Salt and freshly
   ground white pepper

■ Combine all ingedients in a
   closed container and shake
   vigorously until fully mixed.
■ Adjust seasoning.

| PESCE |

CAPPE SANTE AL BURRO CAMPARI
Scallops with Campari Butter

5-2/3 tbsp. (80 mL) sweet butter
1 tsp. (5 mL) shallot, minced
Salt and freshly ground white pepper
40-50 ocean scallops
1 tbsp. (15 mL) dry white wine
2 tbsp. (30 mL) fish stock
1 tsp. (5 mL) fresh lime juice
1 tbsp. (15 mL) Campari
Salt and freshly ground white pepper
6 segments fresh lime, peel and pith removed
12 finely julienned slivers white leek
6 julienned slivers of fresh truffle (optional)

- Gently sauté shallot in 1 tbsp. (15 mL) butter for 2-3 minutes without coloring. Add scallops, lime juice, wine, and fish stock. Bring to boil and, after 10 seconds, remove scallops and set aside (this ensures their staying plump and juicy).
- Reduce liquid in saucepan by half. Add Campari and any juice draining from scallops, and season to taste. Again, reduce liquid by one third. Remove saucepan from heat and swirl in remaining butter without further heating.
- Cover bottom of each warmed serving plate with Campari butter. Scatter scallops to cover entire plate. Garnish with lime segments and juliennes of leek and truffle. Serve immediately with side vegetables of choice.

BRANZINO AL BURRO FINNOCHIO
Sea Bass with Fennel Butter

2-1/2 tbsp. (40 mL) sweet butter

1 black or silver sea bass, about 2 lbs. (1 kg), scaled and fileted

Salt and freshly ground white pepper

Juice of 1/2 lemon

2 oz. (60 g) fresh fennel bulb, julienned

1/2 tsp. (2 mL) shallot, minced

1/4 cup (60 mL) fish stock or clam juice

2 tbsp. (30 mL) dry white wine

4 oz. (115 g) sweet butter, very hard and in 1/2" (1.5 cm) cubes

1/2 tsp. (2 mL) parsley, minced

- Bring 2 tbsp. (30 mL) butter to medium heat in heavy skillet. Season fish with salt, pepper and a dash of lemon juice. Turn heat to very low. Slide fish into skillet skin side down and cook for 10 seconds, shaking skillet from side to side to avoid sticking. Turn fish over and cook for same time without allowing it to brown. Remove from heat and set aside.

- Gently sauté fennel and shallot in 1/2 tbsp. (7 mL) butter until tender, without coloring. Add fish stock, wine, rest of lemon juice and seasoning to taste and reduce to a quarter of volume. Remove saucepan from heat and allow to cool slightly. Add cubes of butter and rotate pan gently until butter has melted and given sauce a velvety texture. Add parsley and set sauce aside without further heating.

- Continue cooking fish for 3-4 minutes more until flesh begins to flake. Transfer to warmed serving platter, cover with butter sauce and serve with appropriate side vegetables.

SALMONE ROSSO IN LATTUGA RAPIENE

Red Spring Salmon in Romaine Lettuce Stuffed with Mussels and Vegetable Julienne

4 centre-cuts Pacific salmon, about 6 oz. (170 g) each, skinned, butterflied and boned
Salt and freshly ground white pepper
20 cooked shelled mussels
4 tbsp. (60 mL) finely julienned mix of rutabaga, leek and carrot, blanched for 30 seconds
4 large leaves Romaine lettuce, very briefly blanched

- Open filets of salmon and season to taste. Stuff each with five mussels and 1 tbsp. (15 mL) of julienned vegetables and reshape to natural form.
- Place each lettuce leaf in turn under some cheesecloth and flatten with side of a cleaver. Place each stuffed filet on a lettuce leaf and fold leaf over to form a neat package. Set aside with fold underneath.
- Melt 1/4 cup (60 mL) butter in baking pan and add

1-1/4 cups (285 mL)
    sweet butter
4 tsp. (20 mL) shallot,
    minced
1/2 cup (120 mL) fish
    stock
1/4 cup (60 mL) dry
    white wine
3/4 tsp. (4 mL) lemon
    juice
1 cup (235 mL) fresh
    grapefruit juice
4 tsp. (20 mL) saffron
    tea*
4 tsp. (20 mL) parsley,
    chopped

shallot. Arrange fish packages in pan and add fish stock, wine and lemon juice, seasoning to taste. Cover with foil and bake in preheated 375°F (190°C) oven for 12-15 minutes. The salmon should be very lightly cooked.

- Remove salmon and keep warm. Set pan on heat and reduce liquid by half, then add grapefruit juice and saffron tea and again reduce by half. Remove pan from heat and whisk in remaining butter. Add parsley just before serving.

- Pat each fish package dry with a paper towel and place at centre of serving plate. Pour a little butter sauce around the fish and garnish with appropriate fresh vegetables.

* SAFFRON TEA: Pour 1/2 cup (120 mL) boiling water over 1 tsp. (5 mL) saffron. Cover and allow to steep until liquid is a deep yellow. Strain and set liquid aside for use.

| CARNE E POLLAME |

ANIMELLE ALLA GRIGLIA CON SALSA DI LIMONE E SALVIA
Grilled Sweetbreads with Lemon and Sage Sauce

2 lbs. (1 kg) veal
  sweetbreads,
  trimmed of any blood
  clots or fat
2-1/2 cups (590 mL)
  rich veal stock
Salt and freshly
  ground white pepper
Bouquet garni
3 tbsp. (45 mL) sweet
  butter
2 tsp. (10 mL) shallot,
  freshly chopped
2/3 tsp. (3 mL) fresh
  sage leaves, chopped
2 pinches cracked
  white peppercorns
Pinch of salt
3 tsp. (15 mL) dry white
  wine
3 tbsp. (45 mL)
  whipping cream
Zest of 2/3 lemon,
  blanched and minced
Vegetable oil

- Poach sweetbreads in veal stock, with salt, pepper and bouquet garni, until they are firm. Allow them to cool in stock. Then remove and discard any excess fat, skin or arteries. Cut on bias into 16 thin slices. Meanwhile, over medium heat, reduce stock by half.
- Briefly sauté shallot in 1/2 tbsp. (7 mL) butter, seasoning with sage, peppercorns and salt. Stir in wine and quickly reduce by half. Add veal stock and reduce by a third.
- Add cream, boil for 1 minute, then strain into a fresh saucepan. Again bring to boil, add lemon zest and remaining butter. Remove from heat and, with an electric hand mixer, aerate sauce; this will lighten it and give it a sheen. Keep warm,

but do not reheat.
- Brush sweetbread slices lightly with vegetable oil, season to taste and grill for about 2 minutes each side, being careful not to overcook.
- Arrange slices on warmed serving plates, lightly cover with 3-4 tbsp. (45-60 mL) of lemon sage sauce. Garnish with suitable fresh vegetables and serve at once.

ROLE DI MANZO
Pinwheel of Beef Tenderloin with Spinach and Smoked Salmon

10-12 oz. (285-340 g) fresh spinach
1 centre-cut beef tenderloin, about 24 oz. (680 g)
2-1/2 oz. (70 g) smoked salmon, very thinly sliced
6 tbsp. (90 mL) vegetable oil
1 tbsp. (15 mL) sweet butter

- Blanch spinach in a little boiling water, squeeze dry in a sieve. Chop and sauté in a little butter, seasoning to taste, for 3 minutes. Allow to cool.
- Lay tenderloin on cutting board. With sharp knife, cut through centre of meat lengthwise to within 1/2" (1.25 cm) of the other side. Open cut tenderloin like a

Salt and freshly
ground black pepper
and nutmeg

4 tbsp. (60 mL) sweet
butter, very hard, cut
in 1/4" (0.6 cm) cubes

2 tbsp. (30 mL) shallot,
minced

3/4 tsp. (4 mL) white
peppercorns, coarsely
crushed

3 sprigs fresh thyme, or
1/2 tsp. (2 mL) dried
thyme

1 small bay leaf

1 pinch fresh rosemary
leaves

2 tbsp. (30 mL) dry
white wine

2 cups (475 mL) strong
veal stock

2 tbsp. (30 mL)
whipping cream

suitcase, with uncut edge
serving as a hinge.

- With uncut hinge as centre,
cover one side of cut
tenderloin with smoked
salmon. Form the spinach as
a ridge lengthwise down
centre of the salmon.

- With salmon-covered side
nearest you, start rolling up
tenderloin, with spinach
forming hub of pinwheel.
When completed it should
resemble a jelly roll. Secure
roll by tying round with
butcher twine every inch (2.5
cm) along its length.

- Brush tied roll with oil and
season. In a little oil, brown
in a roasting pan on all
sides. Roast in a preheated
400°F (205°C) oven for 25
minutes or until sufficiently
tender. Set aside and keep
warm.

- In a sauté pan add roasting
juices to half the butter cubes
and cook shallot with
crushed peppercorns and
herbs without browning.
Add white wine and reduce
by half, then add veal stock

and simmer until reduced a further 10-15%. Strain sauce through cheesecloth into a fresh saucepan, add cream and simmer one minute more. Remove from heat and vigorously whisk in remaining cubes of butter. When blended do not reheat.

— Carefully cut and remove string from tenderloin. Carve into 8 even slices and arrange these 2 to each warm serving plate. Pour a ring of sauce around each serving of meat and garnish with freshly cooked vegetables.

LOMBATO DI VITELLO RIPIENO CON SALSA DI SALVIA
Veal Loin Stuffed with Wild Mushrooms with Sage Sauce

2 lb. (1 kg) loin of veal, trimmed of fat and sinew

2 tbsp. (30 mL) sweet butter

1 tsp. (5 mL) shallot, finely chopped

— Place veal loin flat on table. Cutting in from right-hand edge with sharp knife, make a pocket in loin, leaving about 1/2 inch (1.25 cm) uncut along other three edges.

1 oz. (30 g) dried morels, rinsed and soaked for 15 minutes in warm water
2 oz. (60 g) chantrelles, fresh or canned
2 oz. (60 g) dried porcini mushrooms, rinsed and soaked for 15 minutes in warm water
2 tbsp. (30 mL) brandy
2 tbsp. (30 mL) concentrated brown veal stock
Salt and freshly ground black pepper
1 pinch dried sage

- Gently sauté shallot in butter until soft, add mushrooms coarsely chopped and cook until they begin to soften. Flambé with brandy, season to taste and stir in veal stock. Remove contents from pan and allow to cool.
- Force cool stuffing into pocket in veal loin, making sure that it is evenly spread inside. Pin opening shut with toothpicks. Season outside of veal with salt, pepper and a pinch of dried sage. Place in a small lightly oiled roasting pan and roast in a preheated 350°F (175°C) oven for 20 minutes.

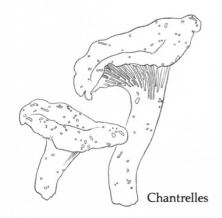

Chantrelles

SALSA DI SALVIA
Sage Sauce

2 tbsp. (30 mL) sweet
  butter
2 tbsp. (30 mL) shallot,
  unpeeled and
  coarsely chopped
1/2 tsp. (2 mL) black
  peppercorns, crushed
Salt
1/3 tsp. (2 mL) fresh
  sage, chopped
1 pinch thyme
1 pinch rosemary
1/2 bay leaf
3 tbsp. (45 mL) dry
  white wine
1-1/4 cups (285 mL)
  concentrated veal
  stock
4 tbsp. (60 mL)
  whipping cream
2 tbsp. (30 mL) cold
  sweet butter

- When meat is cooked, remove from pan and keep warm. Drain fat from pan, replace with butter and sauté shallot, with peppercorns and salt to taste, until shallot begins to color slightly. Add herbs and cook for 1 minute, making sure they do not burn.
- Add wine and raise heat while scraping any meat particles from pan with a wooden spoon, then add veal stock and simmer very slowly for about 20 minutes.
- Add cream and continue to simmer sauce until it begins to thicken. Adjust seasoning. Strain through fine sieve or cheesecloth into a clean sauté pan. Reheat without boiling and glaze by quickly whisking in cold butter until it is absorbed.
- Serve thin slices of stuffed veal with sauce around edge of plate. Accompany with suitable fresh vegetables.

POLLO AI FERRI CON POMODORI FRESCA
Grilled Chicken with Tomato Relish

2 free-range chickens, about 2 lbs (1 kg) each

6 cloves garlic, thinly sliced

3 tbsp. (45 mL) fresh thyme leaves

1 tbsp. (15 mL) fresh rosemary

1 tbsp. (15 mL) parsley, chopped coarsely

1 tbsp. (15 mL) freshly ground white peppercorns

1/4 tsp. (1.2 mL) hot green chile, minced

1 tsp. (5 mL) sugar

Juice of 1 lemon

6 tbsp. (90 mL) vegetable oil mixed with 1 tsp. (5 mL) Dijon mustard

3 large vine tomatoes, peeled, seeded and cut in small cubes

1 small red onion, very finely diced

4 tbsp. (60 mL) virgin olive oil

- Cut chickens in half and bone carefully, retaining shape of breasts and legs, leaving intact only first joint of wing bone.
- Thoroughly mix together garlic slices, thyme, rosemary, parsley, peppercorns and chile, and rub over surface of chicken halves. Blend together sugar, lemon juice, oil and mustard and drizzle over all sides of chicken. Leave to marinate in a pan for at least 6 hours, turning and basting occasionally.
- Before cooking chicken, make relish by combining tomato and onion with oil, lemon juice, vinegar, garlic and seasoning to taste. Set this aside.
- Drain excess marinade from chicken halves and grill them 10 minutes each side, being careful not to overcook. Dry chicken with

Juice of 1 lemon
l tbsp. (15 mL) red wine
   vinegar
1/2 tsp. (2 mL) garlic,
   minced
Salt and freshly
   ground white pepper
   and nutmeg

paper towel when cooked. Serve immediately with fresh tomato relish in place of sauce. As side vegetable, serve grilled zucchini (see below).

ZUCCHINI AI FERRI
Grilled Zucchini

4 small zucchini
1 tbsp. (15 mL)
   vegetable oil
1/2 tsp. (2 mL) garlic,
   minced
Salt and freshly
   ground white pepper
   and nutmeg

- Cut zucchini in half lengthwise. Blanch in boiling salted water for 45 seconds, then refresh in iced water.
- Dress zucchini with oil, garlic and seasoning to taste. Grill flat side down for 5 minutes or until cooked.
- Coincide cooking to that of chicken and serve at same time.

$\boxed{\text{D O L C E}}$

PANNA E BACCE FRESCO IN SFOGLIA

Cream and Fresh Berries in Phyllo Pastry

6 sheets phyllo pastry
1/4 cup (60 mL) sweet
   butter, melted
1 egg yolk, whipped in
   1 tbsp. (15 mL) cold
   water
Sugar
Ground cinnamon
2 cups (475 mL) fresh
   berries (raspberries,
   blackberries or
   strawberries, as
   available)
1-1/2 cups (355 mL)
   whipping cream
2 tbsp. (30 mL) sugar
1/4 tsp. (1.2 mL) grated
   lemon zest
1 tsp. (5 mL) fresh mint,
   finely chopped
1 tbsp. (15 mL) icing
   sugar
6 egg yolks
2 tbsp. (30 mL) fresh
   lemon juice
2 tbsp. (30 mL) white
   wine

■ Keep phyllo pastry sheets
under damp cloth until
needed. Spread one sheet on
counter and brush lightly
with melted butter. Then
lightly brush over with egg
wash. Spread a second sheet
over first and brush with
butter and egg wash. Then
spread a third sheet on top
of these and brush with
butter only.

■ With a 3" (7.5 cm) round
cookie cutter, cut eight discs
from piled phyllo sheets and
set aside on a greased
floured baking sheet.

■ Repeat the operation with
the three remaining phyllo
sheets. You will then have 16
pastry discs on baking
sheets. Sprinkle the leftover
scraps of pastry with sugar
and cinnamon and set scraps
on edge of baking sheets.

■ In a preheated 350°F (175°C)
oven, bake pastry for 5-8

4 tbsp. (60 mL) sugar
1 tbsp. (15 mL)
  Drambuie
8 sprigs fresh mint

minutes or until golden brown. If necessary, turn baking sheets in oven to ensure even browning. When fully cooked, set pastries on wire racks to cool.

- Reserve eight berries for garnish. But if using strawberries, rinse them briefly, remove hulls and slice in half lengthwise.
- Whip cream until it begins to thicken. Blend in sugar, lemon zest and mint and beat until cream is firm.
- Set out on counter 12 baked discs, keeping aside discs brushed with butter only. With piping bag or spoon, spread whipped cream on each disc. Make a circle of berries (strawberries hulled and halved) round the rim of each cream-covered disc and fill the middle space with a little more cream. Using four discs as base, pile two more covered discs on top, pressing down lightly. Top off each of four piles with a plain disc and dust with icing sugar. Set out on

CACIOTTA DI CAPRA AL PEPE
Goat Cheese with Peppercorns
PRONTO – PAGE 113

ROLE DI MANZO
**Pinwheel of Beef Tenderloin with
Spinach and Smoked Salmon**
PRONTO – PAGE 120

STRACCIATELLE
Egg and Cheese Broth
SAN LORENZO – PAGE 138

POLLO AL FORNO DELLA NONNA
Grandmother's Roast Chicken
SAN LORENZO – PAGE 148

four serving plates.
- In a double saucepan or a
  bowl over simmering water,
  whisk together egg yolks,
  lemon juice, wine, sugar and
  Drambuie until mixture
  becomes velvety smooth,
  about 30 to 60 seconds.
  Remove from heat and
  spoon puddles of sauce
  around phyllo piles on
  plates. Garnish with
  reserved berries, mint leaves
  and baked scraps of pastry.

BORSELLINO DELLA MELE
Purse of Apples

4 rectangles of puff
  pastry dough, 1/4" x
  5-1/2" x 3-1/2" (0.5 cm
  x 15 cm x 10 cm)
3 Northern Spy apples,
  peeled, cored and cut
  in 1/4" (0.5 cm) slices,
  rubbed with lemon
  juice to keep white
Granulated sugar
1 tbsp. (15 mL) sweet
  butter
1 egg, well beaten
Icing sugar

- Score a ridge round pastry
  1/4" (0.5 cm) in from edge,
  just barely scoring the
  surface of dough. This will
  provide edge to contain fruit
  at centre when baked.
- Arrange apple slices
  overlapping to cover centre
  of pastry, but do not overlap
  marked edge. Sprinkle
  apples lightly with
  granulated sugar and dot
  with flakes of butter.
- Very lightly brush uncovered

edge with egg wash and
bake the purses in a
preheated 450°F (230°C)
oven for 15-18 minutes or
until apples have softened
and pastry has turned
golden brown.
- Remove from oven, dust
surface lightly with icing
sugar and place under
broiler for a few moments to
melt and caramelize icing
sugar and give tarts a
lacquered sheen. Keep warm
until ready to serve.

Pronto Recommended Wines

BIANCHI
Clastidium Reserva
Ribolla Gialla (Fabio Berin)
Pinot Grigio (Bertoluzzi '77)

ROSSI
Barbaresco (Gaja '73)
Amarone della Valpolicella
Barolo (Giacomo Ascheri '74)

San Lorenzo

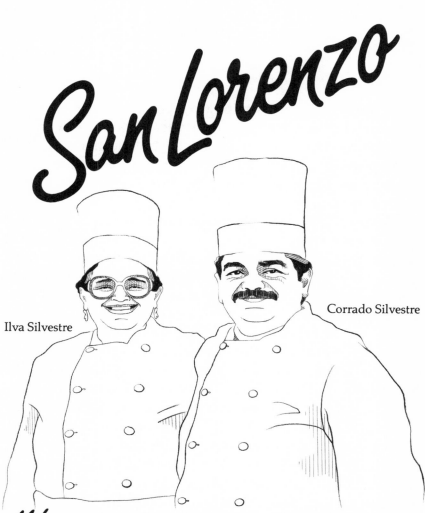

Ilva Silvestre

Corrado Silvestre

IN appearance the restaurant conforms exactly with the surviving Victorian elegance and dignity of the stretch of King Street on which it stands, an effect heightened by the graceful sculpture garden set to one side of it.

The big uncurtained lattice windows around its doorway are inviting, and the invitation seems to have been very well worth accepting once you step inside. To the right is a counter topped by a lighted showcase exhibiting freshly made antipasti and desserts. To the left, up a short flight of steps, is a long bar for those who wish to dally or who are waiting for a vacant table. Ahead the sense of roomy charm is enhanced by another stairway, leading to an airy upstairs dining room; behind it, is the downstairs room, enlivened by large and colorful abstract originals.

Yet despite its high style, the San Lorenzo is in its operation an authentic family restaurant. From the open kitchen that faces the bar behind the showcases, you are very likely to be welcomed by its chef and co-owner Corrado Silvestri or to see his mother, Ilva Silvestri, performing Northern Italian miracles at the stove.

Earlier in his international career, Silvestri might have been welcoming you as maitre d' or manager, since his early training and experience were in front-of-house operations. But in Italy his mother had cooked professionally and that had inspired in him a longing to cook. In 1982, not long after the family had settled in Toronto, the opportunity to do so arose when he and a partner took the plunge and opened on King Street East. It was not, he admits ruefully, the ideal time to open a new restaurant. A temporary recession had struck and more restaurants were closing than opening in the city. But the family, for his mother still actively cooks until 7 p.m. every day, persevered and triumphed.

The choice of location, if not the timing, was acute. While close to major downtown hotels, to the Bay Street business and Front Street theatre hubs, King Street East at that point manages to suggest a soothing seclusion from the hustle of downtown. Business and theatre people, politicians and knowledgeable visitors to the city have recognized the place as a beguiling oasis in which to relax and talk. And, of course, in which to eat well. Near the bar is a large color photograph, taken in the restaurant in 1985, showing the celebrated tenor Luciano Pavarotti with Silvestri; both are large men who look as though they know how to do justice to fine food.

Ristorante San Lorenzo has earned a quite enviable reputation for the authentic quality of its Italian regional cuisine, based largely on the specialties of the Piedmont and Emilia-Romagna regions where the family has its roots: butter is used more often than olive oil, extra-virgin olive oil where it counts, pasta made in house by rolling (not extrusion), genuine Parmeggiano cheese and well-aged balsamic vinegar. Indeed Silvestri is so proud

of his pasta and balsamic vinegar (a brother in Italy nurtures his supply) that he will sell some to you to use in your own cooking. It is a wise and worthwhile first step, however, to taste what the Silvestris can make of such delicacies before you try to yourself.

RISTORANTE SAN LORENZO, 125 King Street East. Telephone: 366-2556. Lunch served from noon to 3 p.m. Monday to Friday; dinner served from 5.30 p.m to 11 p.m. Monday to Thursday, and until 11.30 p.m. Friday and Saturday. Closed on Sundays and all statutory holidays. Fully licensed. Major cards accepted. Reservations recommended.

$$\boxed{\text{A N T I P A S T I}}$$

MELANZANE AI FERRI
Grilled Eggplant

3 medium eggplants
Salt
1 tbsp. (15 mL)
  vegetable oil
3 fresh hot peppers
Olive oil

- Peel eggplants and cut in slices 1 inch (2.5 cm) thick. Sprinkle well with salt on both sides and leave for 4 hours on a wire rack at room temperature.
- Thoroughly rinse all remaining salt from slices under running cold water and return to rack to dry for 4 hours more at room temperature.
- Heat a heavy cast-iron skillet over a strong flame, and allow to become very hot. Brush both sides of each eggplant slice lightly with vegetable oil and cook one at a time, slightly browning each side, for about 45 seconds.
- Set slices back on rack to cool. Then put in a large jar in layers, with slices of hot pepper and olive oil between each layer, ensuring that the top layer is covered by oil. If possible, allow to marinate for at least a month before serving as an antipasto.

ZUCCHINI ANTIPASTO

4-5 tbsp. (60-75 mL)
  olive oil
1 clove garlic, chopped
1 lb. (455 g) zucchini cut
  in 2" (5 cm) strips
1 Spanish onion,
  chopped
2 tbsp. (30 mL)
  balsamic vinegar

- Quickly heat oil in heavy sauté pan and cook garlic until it begins to brown. Remove garlic and discard.
- Over strong heat, quickly sauté zucchini strips, without scorching and remove to a bowl.
- Pour off all but 1 tbsp. (15 mL) of oil and sauté onion for 30 seconds, then swirl in vinegar and pour over zucchini.
- Put antipasto in refrigerator to chill. Mix well before serving.

INSALATE

INSALATA RUSSA
Russian Salad

2 large potatoes
2 medium carrots
7 oz. (200 g) green
  peas, fresh if
  available
5 oz. (140 g) pickled
  cornichons
3/4 cup (175 mL) lemon
  mustard mayonnaise
Salt and freshly
  ground black pepper
1 dash of balsamic
  vinegar

- Simmer unpeeled potatoes amd scrubbed carrots separately until cooked but still firm. Cook peas very lightly.
- When vegetables have cooled, peel potatoes and cut into small cubes; also cube carrots. Chop cornichons coarsely.
- Put all cooked ingredients and mayonnaise, with seasoning and vinegar to taste, in a large bowl and gently handmix them together until vegetables are evenly coated. Chill before serving.

INSALATA DI MANISCALCO
Blacksmith's Salad

1 head radicchio
  lettuce
1-1/2 cups (355 mL)
  Parmesan cheese, cut
  in slivers
Salt
4 tbsp. (60 mL)
  balsamic vinegar
Extra-virgin olive oil

- Tear radicchio into bite-size pieces. Toss with cheese, a little salt and vinegar until cheese darkens.
- Add oil to taste and allow to stand for 20 minutes before serving.

ZUPPE

STRACCIATELLE
Egg and Cheese Broth

4 cups (945 mL) veal
  stock (see page 147)
Salt
2 eggs
3/4 cup (175 mL)
  Parmesan cheese,
  freshly ground
1 pinch nutmeg

— Bring stock to boil,
  seasoning carefully, since
  cheese will increase
  saltiness.
— In a bowl, whisk together
  eggs, cheese and nutmeg.
  Slowly pour into this a ladle
  of hot stock, continuing to
  whisk until thoroughly
  mixed.
— Blend mixture into boiling
  stock and immediately
  remove from heat. Serve at
  once.

MINESTRONE NOSTRANO
Mixed Vegetable Soup

1/2 cup (120 mL) sweet
  butter
1 celery stalk, chopped
1/2 medium onion,
  chopped
2 large potatoes,
  peeled and cubed
1 carrot, cubed
1 lb. (455 g) assorted
  available mixed

— In a large saucepan melt
  butter and sauté celery and
  onion, then add potato and
  carrot and continue to sauté
  gently for 7 minutes. Add
  half the stock and simmer
  until vegetables are almost
  cooked.
— Add remaining stock and
  bring to a simmer, then add

vegetables, coarsely chopped.
4 cups (945 mL) veal stock (see page 147)
1/2 cup (120 mL) Parmesan cheese, grated

other vegetables and simmer until cooked but still firm. Season to taste.
- Sprinkle each serving of soup with cheese, and offer additional cheese at table.

ZUPPA DI PATATE
Potato Soup

1/2 cup (120 mL) sweet butter
1 medium onion, chopped
1 stalk celery, chopped
3 large sweet potatoes, peeled and cubed
3 large potatoes, peeled and cubed
4 cups (945 mL) veal stock (see page 147)
Salt and freshly ground black pepper
1/2 cup (120 mL) Parmesan cheese
Whipping cream (optional)

- In a large heavy saucepan, sauté onion and celery in butter until they begin to soften. Add both kinds of potatoes and sauté over medium heat, stirring occasionally, for 7 minutes.
- Add half the veal stock and simmer until vegetables are cooked. Add more stock, but allow soup to remain thick. Season to taste.
- Sprinkle each serving with cheese, offering additional cheese at table. If left to cool overnight and then skimmed of excess fat, the soup can be puréed and served cold, enriched by the addition of a little whipping cream.

RISI E PASTA

RISOTTO NERO AL BALSAMICO

1/2 cup (120 mL) sweet
  butter
1/2 onion, chopped
1 bay leaf
1 pinch dried rosemary
1-1/4 cups (285 mL)
  Arborio rice
2-1/2 cups (590 mL)
  chicken stock
1-1/4 cup (285 mL) red
  wine, preferably
  Barolo
1/2 cup (120 mL)
  Parmesan cheese,
  grated
6 tbsp. (90 mL)
  balsamic vinegar

- Melt half the butter in a large sauté pan and lightly cook onion, bay leaf and rosemary. Add rice and sauté for one minute, stirring well.
- Add stock and bring to boil, then add wine and stir well. Simmer gently, uncovered, until almost all liquid is absorbed.
- Incorporate remaining butter and the cheese and continue cooking for 3-4 minutes. Just before serving, gently mix in vinegar.

LUMANCHE SAN LORENZO
Snails in Pasta

3 tbsp. (45 mL) sweet
  butter
1 medium onion, finely
  chopped
1 bay leaf
1 clove garlic, lightly
  crushed

- In a heavy sauté pan, fry onion, bay leaf and garlic until onion becomes transparent. Add wine and parsley and continue to simmer until liquid is reduced. Discard garlic and bay leaf, add escargots and 2

3 tbsp. (45 mL) dry
  white wine
1/2 cup (120 mL)
  parsley, finely
  chopped
18 large canned French
  escargots, with juice
Salt and freshly
  ground black pepper
Cayenne
1 tbsp. (15 mL)
  sambucca
1-1/2 tbsp. (20 mL)
  bechamel sauce (see
  page 149)
18 sheets fresh pasta,
  4" (10 cm) square,
  cooked al dente
1-1/4 cups (285 mL)
  whipping cream
2 tbsp. (30 mL) tomato
  concasse (thick raw
  paste of skinned and
  seeded tomato)

tbsp. (30 mL) of their juice,
season to taste with salt,
pepper and cayenne, then
mix in sambucca and simmer
for 2 minutes more.

- Remove sauce from heat
  and allow to cool to room
  temperature. Blend with
  bechamel sauce.
- Lay each pasta square in
  turn on counter, put an
  escargot and a little sauce in
  centre, fold corners of pasta
  to centre to form a package,
  then place with folded side
  down in a clean sauté pan.
- When all the escargots are
  wrapped, pour enough
  cream in pan to leave a third
  of each package uncovered,
  blend in tomato concasse
  and season to taste. Simmer
  gently until sauce begins to
  thicken.
- Serve immediately in heated
  bowls with plenty of cream
  sauce.

FETTUCCINE MODO MIO

1-1/2 cups (355 mL) whipping cream

1-1/2 cups (355 mL) Parmesan cheese, freshly ground

1 lb. (455 g) fresh fettuccine

4 egg yolks

2 tsp. (10 g) preserved green peppercorns with juice

- In a heavy sauté pan, cook cream and 3/4 of cheese (265 mL) until it begins to thicken.
- Meanwhile, in plenty of boiling salted water, cook fettuccine until al dente. Drain thoroughly.
- Add fettuccine to simmering cream sauce and mix well. Remove from heat and then completely blend in the egg yolks, peppercorns and juice.
- Serve hot, with remaining cheese sprinkled on top.

FETTUCCINE IOLANDA

7 tbsp. (100 mL) sweet butter

1 clove garlic, slightly crushed

1 small fresh hot red pepper

10 oz. (285 g) fresh leaf spinach

12 oz. (340 g) fresh fettuccine

4 oz. (115 g) prosciutto, finely julienned

- Briefly sauté garlic and red pepper in 5 tbsp. (70 mL) butter. Add spinach, rinsed but not shaken dry. Cover and cook very briefly. Discard garlic and pepper and purée the spinach.
- Meanwhile cook fettuccine al dente in plenty of boiling salted water and drain well. Lightly sauté prosciutto in remaining butter, blend with

3 tbsp. (45 mL)
  whipping cream
Black pepper, freshly
  ground
Parmesan cheese,
  freshly grated

puréed spinach and cream.
Combine with fettuccine,
mixing thoroughly.
- Serve at once, garnished
  with ground pepper and
  cheese.

SCAMPI GIULIA

5 tbsp. (70 mL) sweet
  butter
1 clove garlic, crushed
24 large shrimps, raw,
  peeled and deveined
Salt and freshly
  ground black pepper
1/4 cup (60 mL) dry
  white wine
2 level tbsp. (30 mL)
  pesto (see page 151)
12-13 oz. (340-370 g)
  fresh tagliolini
3 tbsp. (45 mL) pine
  nuts

- Melt butter in large sauté
  pan and fry garlic until it
  begins to color, then discard
  it. Lightly fry shrimps in
  butter, seasoning to taste.
  When they turn pink add
  wine and pesto and sauté
  for 1 minute. Remove
  shrimps and keep warm.
- Meanwhile cook tagliolini al
  dente in plenty of boiling
  salted water. When cooked,
  drain well and mix with
  pesto sauce.
- Turn pasta into very hot
  serving platter, display
  shrimp on top and sprinkle
  with pine nuts before
  serving.

$$\boxed{\text{P E S C E}}$$

Trota in Carpione
Marinated Trout

4 fresh trout, about 6 oz. (170 g) each, with head on
Flour
6 tbsp. (90 mL) vegetable oil
1 medium onion, thinly sliced
2 cloves garlic, crushed
3 sprigs fresh sage
3 tbsp. (45 mL) balsamic vinegar
2/3 cup (155 mL) red wine vinegar
Salt and freshly ground black pepper

- Rinse trout well, dry with a tea towel and leave to dry on towel for 30 minutes.
- Coat trout with flour, shaking off any excess. Heat oil in a sauté pan and fry fish lightly, one at a time. Allow fish to cool slighly on a wire rack.
- In a separate pan, sauté onion, garlic and sage in a little oil until onion is transparent. Add both vinegars and cook over medium heat until liquid is reduced by half.
- Lay fish in shallow dish, strain hot marinade over them and refrigerate for 12 hours before serving as a cold dish.

FETTUCCINE GIAN CARLO

3 tbsp. (45 mL) extra-virgin olive oil
1/2 medium onion, finely chopped
1 clove garlic, crushed
1 tbsp. (15 mL) chopped parsley
4 tbsp. (60 mL) tomato sauce (see page 149)
6 tbsp. (90 mL) dry white wine
4 scampi (or large prawns), raw, peeled, deveined and butterflied
24 cultured mussels, scrubbed and bearded
12 shrimps, raw, peeled and deveined
12 large scallops
Salt and freshly ground black pepper
1/2 lb. (225 g) fresh fettuccine

- Heat oil in large sauté pan and cook onion, garlic and parsley until onion begins to color. Add tomato sauce and wine, bring to simmer and cook scampi and mussels until mussels open. Season shrimps and scallops to taste meanwhile and add these to sauce to cook for 3-4 minutes.
- In plenty of boiling salted water, cook fettuccine until al dente and drain well. Remove seafood from sauce, discard garlic and thoroughly coat pasta with sauce.
- Turn pasta and sauce into a warmed serving dish, arrange seafood on top and serve very hot.

| CARNE E POLLAME |

SCALOPPINI DI VITELLO CON FINOCCHIO
Veal with Fennel

1/2 bulb fresh fennel
3 tbsp. (45 mL) sweet
  butter, softened
3 tbsp. (45 mL) flour
Salt and freshly
  ground white pepper
1 lb. (455 g) Provimi
  veal, cut into 16
  scaloppini, beaten
  very thin
1/2 cup (120 mL) white
  wine
1 cup (235 mL)
  whipping cream

- Clip green leaves from fennel and set aside. Steam fennel over a little boiling water until tender. When cool cut into 1/4 inch (0.5 cm) juliennes.
- Heat 1 tbsp. (15 mL) butter in sauté pan. Lightly flour and season scaloppini. Sauté 10 seconds each side and keep warm.
- Add remaining butter and fennel to pan, then white wine. Loosen any sediment from bottom of pan, add cream, seasoning to taste, and allow to thicken slightly.
- Spoon some fennel and sauce over each serving and garnish with finely minced green from fennel. Serve with appropriate side vegetables.

BRODO DI VITELLO
Veal Stock

---

1 large veal bone,
  sawn up
1 chicken carcass
1 small onion
1 celery stalk
1 medium carrot,
  scrubbed
1 small ripe tomato
1 chicken broth cube
14 cups (3.5 L) water
1/3 tsp. (1.5 mL) whole
  black peppercorns

- Put all ingredients in water in a stock pot and bring to boil, skimming off any foam. Simmer for 4 hours.
- Strain through fine sieve or cheesecloth. Stock will keep refrigerated in an air-tight container for at least 10 days, and longer if again brought to boil and rechilled. It may also be frozen and stored.

POLLO AL FORNO DELLA NONNA
Grandmother's Roast Chicken

2 small roasting
    chickens
1 tbsp. (15 mL) Dijon
    mustard
1 tbsp. (15 mL) olive oil
1 clove garlic, crushed
1 sprig fresh rosemary
    or 1/2 tsp. (2 mL)
    dried rosemary
1/2 cup (120 mL) dry
    white wine
3 tbsp. (45 mL)
    balsamic vinegar
Salt and freshly
    ground black pepper

- Quarter chickens, discarding end sections of wings and backbone. Mix together remaining ingredients, seasoning to taste.
- Rub some of marinade into each quarter of chicken, then put chicken in a bowl, cover with remaining marinade and refrigerate for 8 hours, turning over pieces every hour or so.
- Preheat oven to 450°F (230°C). Shake chicken quarters free of excess marinade, lay in a single layer in a large baking pan. Cook for 10 minutes, then lower oven heat to 375°F (190°C) and cook for a further 10 minutes. Turn chicken quarters over and continue cooking until done but not dried out, about 15 minutes more.
- A radicchio salad, dressed with balsamic vinegar and olive oil, makes a perfect accompaniment for the chicken.

SALSA BESCIAMELLA
Bechamel Sauce

7 tbsp. (100 mL) sweet butter
6 tbsp. (90 mL) flour
4-1/4 cups (1 L) milk
Salt and freshly ground nutmeg

- Melt butter in heavy saucepan, dredge in flour and stir into butter and cook gently for 4-5 minutes without browning.
- Bring milk to boil, then add all at once to butter and flour. Remove from heat and whisk until fully incorporated. Return to heat and bring to boil, then simmer for 4-5 minutes, stirring frequently. Season with a pinch each of salt and nutmeg and set aside.

SALSA DI POMODORO ALL'ILVA
Ilva's Tomato Sauce

7 tbsp. (100 mL) sweet butter
4 tbsp. (60 mL) extra-virgin olive oil
1 onion, finely chopped
2 celery stalks, finely chopped
2 garlic cloves, crushed
3-4 fresh basil leaves,

- In a large heavy saucepan, sauté onion, celery, garlic and basil in butter and oil until onion looks transparent. Discard garlic. Crush tomatoes with hands as they are added to saucepan, season to taste and add red pepper as sauce is brought

chopped, or 1 tbsp. (15 mL) dried basil
48 oz. (1.36 kg) canned plum tomatoes (San Marzano brand if available)
1 hot red pepper
Salt

to a simmer.
- Cook very slowly, uncovered, for about 2 hours until surface of sauce has a mirror-like sheen. This sauce has many uses and will keep, refrigerated in a closed container, for 7-10 days.

RAGU DI FAGIOLI
Bean Sauce

2 lbs. (1 kg) dried Romano beans
5 oz. (140 g) piece prosciutto, with rind on
5 tbsp. (75 mL) sweet butter
2 celery stalks, finely chopped
1 large onion, finely chopped
1 cup (235 mL) Ilva's Tomato Sauce (see above)
Salt and freshly ground black pepper

- Wash beans and discard any impurities. Soak overnight in plenty of cold water.
- Discard soaking water and simmer beans in 9 cups (2 L) water until almost cooked, still firm to touch. Drain but reserve cooking water.
- In another large saucepan, sauté celery and onion in butter until soft. Add beans, tomato sauce and reserved cooking water. Simmer gently until beans are soft.
- This ragu can be served with pasta or, diluted by veal stock, will serve as a hearty soup. Frozen serving portions in closed containers can be stored indefinitely.

PESTO
Basil Paste

2-1/4 lbs. (1 kg) fresh basil leaves (no flower tops)

2 tbsp. (30 mL) extra-virgin olive oil

3 tbsp. (45 mL) Parmesan cheese, freshly grated

1-1/2 tbsp. (20 mL) Romano cheese, freshly grated

2 medium cloves garlic, peeled

1-1/2 tbsp. (20 mL) unsalted cashew nuts

1-1/2 tbsp. (20 mL) pine nuts

Salt and freshly ground black pepper

- Wash basil leaves thoroughly in several changes of water, discarding any remaining stalks. Shake off moisture, then dry completely with a tea towel.
- Combine all ingredients, except nuts, in a food processor, seasoning lightly since cheese is quite salty. Process until reduced to paste. Add cashew nuts and process briefly, leaving them coarse. Turn pesto into a bowl and thoroughly mix in pine nuts.
- Pesto can be used as dressing for pasta and seafood. 1 level tsp. (5 mL) is an adequate single serving. If frozen in closed containers, preferably in small serving portions, it can be kept indefinitely. Once unfrozen, it will deteriorate in a few days.

$$\boxed{\text{D O L C E}}$$

Most of San Lorenzo's desserts are specially created by Flavia Locchi, whose GENEL PATISSERIE at 1137 Queen Street East in Toronto provides pastries, cakes and desserts to shoppers and by special order. Telephone: (416) 463-9768. The following recipe is based on a GENEL dessert.

ZABAGLIONE GATEAU

1 square sponge cake
1 round sponge cake
Marsala
4 tbsp. (60 mL) sugar
1/4 cup (60 mL) water
6 egg yolks
1/2 cup (120 mL) sugar
2 tbsp. (30 mL) water
4 egg whites
1-1/2 tbsp. (20 mL) gelatin
3 tbsp. (45 mL) water
2 cups (475 mL) whipping cream, beaten stiff
6 tbsp. (90 mL) Marsala

— Assemble and lightly butter a 10" (25 cm) round spring-form cake mold. Cut square sponge cake into thin slices and line sides of mold, trimming edges level with top. Cut round sponge cake in half horizontally. Trim one half to fit snugly into bottom of mold. Paint sponge lining with Marsala until thoroughly soaked.

— Bring 4 tbsp. (60 mL) sugar and 1/4 cup water (60 mL) to boil in a small pan. Over boiling water in a double-saucepan, whisk egg yolks until they become light and fluffy, then beat in boiling sugar and water and continue whisking until mixture begins to thicken. Remove from heat and continue whisking until mixture cools.

- In another small saucepan, stir 1/2 cup (120 mL) sugar into 2 tbsp. (30 mL) water and heat to 250°F (120°C). Meanwhile soak gelatine in water to soften. Whisk egg whites until stiff. Into this blend hot sugar mixture and soaked gelatin, continuing to whisk until cool.
- Gently fold together the two prepared mixtures. When they are well mixed, fold in Marsala and whipped cream.
- Pour half the mixture into the lined cake mold, on top of filling lay trimmed second half of round sponge cake, then pour in the remainder of mixure and smooth it. Seal with plastic wrap and chill for at least 4 hours before serving.
- To serve, remove from spring mold and set on a serving plate. Decorate with whipped cream and/or chocolate shavings. Cut in wedges.

FRAGOLE BALSAMICO
Balsamic Strawberries

1 lb. (455 g) fresh
  strawberries
3 tbsp. (45 mL)
  balsamic vinegar
Sugar

- Rinse, hull and dry the berries. If large, cut in halves.
- Put in a bowl, sprinkle with vinegar, turning over gently. Let stand for 15 minutes. Add sugar, turn over again. Serve at once.

San Lorenzo Recommended Wines

BIANCHI
Cortese di Gavi
Verdicchio dei Castelli di Jesi
Pinot Grigio (Grave de Fruili)

ROSSI
Masi Campo Fiorin
Chianti Classico (La Massa)*
Vino Nobile di Montepulciano

* Liquor Licensing Board of Ontario Vintages stock; the other wines are obtainable in most LCBO stores.

GLOSSARY OF ITALIAN TERMS

Acciughe - anchovies. Also alici

Aceto - vinegar

Acqua minerale - mineral water

Affumicato - smoked

Agnello - lamb

Agro - sour

Agrodolce - sweet-sour

Arrosto - roast

Basilico - basil

Besciamella - bechamel

in Bianco - simply cooked

Bistecca - rib steak

Bollito - boiled

Bollito misto - mixture of various meats boiled and often served with salsa verde (see page 156)

Brodetto - Adriatic seafood soup; usually cooked seafood and broth are served separately but at same time

Brodo - broth

Bruscetta - oven-toasted bread dressed with oil and garlic

al Burro - cooked in butter

Caldo - warm, hot

Capocollo - salt-cured neck of pork

Carciofi - artichokes

Carciofini - artichoke hearts

Carpaccio - wafers of lean raw beef dressed with mustard or oil-lemon sauce

della Casa - of the house (restaurant)

Cipolle - onions

Cozze - mussels

Crostini - small toasted or fried slices of bread with savoury topping

Dolce - sweet, dessert

Fagioli - white beans

Farcito - stuffed

Farfalle - butterfly-shaped pasta

Fegatini - chicken liver

Fegato - liver

ai Ferri - grilled on iron grid; barbecued

Finocchio - fennel

Freddo - cold

Fresco - fresh

Fritto - fried

Fritto misto di mare - various seafood boiled and deep-fried

Frutti di mare - seafood

al Funghetto - cooked in hot oil

Funghi - mushrooms and wild fungus

Gelato - ice cream

del Giorno - of the day

alla Griglia - grilled

Latte - milk

Manzo - beef

Melanzane - eggplants

Mele - apples

Misto - mixed

Mortadella - large sausage of cooked pork originating from Bologna

Mozzarella - cow's milk cheese: hard variety used in cooking; softer kind used in both cooking and at table; and smoked as appetizer or dessert

Noci - walnuts

Oca - goose
Occhio di bue - fried egg
(means "ox eye")
Olio di oliva - olive oil
Origano - oregano
Osso buco alla milanese -
knuckle of veal, including
marrow, cooked in wine and
tomato sauce

Panata - pancake of bread, eggs,
cheese and nutmeg served
floating in hot broth
Pane - bread
Panna - cream
Panna montata - whipped
cream
Panzarotti - deep-fried
crescents of pizza dough
stuffed with cheese mixture
Parmigiana - sauce or dish
containing Parmesan cheese
Pepe - pepper
Peperoncini - chile peppers
Peperoni - bell peppers
Pere - pears
Pesce - fish
Pesto - uncooked dressing of
fresh basil, garlic, pine nuts,
sardo or Parmesan cheese,
and olive oil originating
from Genoa
Pinoli - pine nuts
Pizzaiola - sauce of fresh
tomatoes, oregano or basil
and garlic for meat, common
in Naples
Pollo - chicken
Polpette - meatballs
Pomodoro - tomato

Porcini - wild mushrooms;
cepes
Primavera - raw spring
vegetables dressed with garlic
and olive oil
Prosciutto - smoked ham that
is usually, but not invariably,
preserved uncooked

Ricotta - fresh soft cheese,
properly made from ewe's
milk, but cow's milk often
substituted
Ripieno - stuffed
Riso - rice

Salsa - sauce
Salsa verde - uncooked sauce
of minced parsley, capers,
juice, olive oil and salt and
pepper, sometimes with
anchovy added, served with
either fish or meat
Secco - dry
Spumone - soft ice cream
Stracciatella - beef or chicken
broth garnished with
mixture of egg and cheese
Stufato - braised or stewed
Sugo - sauce

Tartufi - truffles

Vitello - veal
Vongole - clams

Zuppa - soup
Zuppa inglese - trifle

INDEX

ANTIPASTI
ANTIPASTO CALDO SAN GIACOMO Warm Seafood Salad, 26
COZZE ALLA MARINARA Steamed Mussels with Tomato Sauce, 25
COZZE CON CREMA E BASILICA Mussels with Fresh Basil Cream, 108
COZZE CON PANCHETTA, FINOCCHIO E PANNA Mussels with Bacon, Fennel and Cream, 77
COZZE IN BRODETTO Mussels in Sauce, 52
FIORI DI ZUCCHINI FRITTI Deep-Fried Stuffed Zucchini Flowers, 78
FRITTATA Open-Face Omelette, 54
GAMBERI FRA DIAVOLO Shrimp Fra Diavolo, 53
INSALATA DI FRUTTI DI MARE Seafood Salad, 24
MELANZANE AI FERRI Grilled Eggplant, 135
MOZZARELLA POMODORI E PROSCIUTTO CALDI Baked Cheese with Tomato and Prosciutto, 53
RADICCHIO E FUNGHI AI FERRI Grilled Radicchio and Oyster Mushrooms, 76
SAN GIACOMO DRESSING (for antipasto), 26
ZUCCHINI AL TIMO Zucchini with Thyme, 107
ZUCCHINI ANTIPASTO, 136

DESERTS
BORSELLINO DELLA MELE Purse of Apples, 129
Crème Fraîche, 45
FRAGOLE AL VINO ROSSO Strawberries in Red Wine, 70
FRAGOLE BALSAMICO Balsamic Strawberries, 154
IL DIPLOMATICO Rum and Coffee Flavored Chocolate Layer Cake, 99
LINZER DOUGH, 47
PANNA E BACCE FRESCO IN SFOGLIA Cream and Fresh Berries in Phyllo Pastry, 127

SPUMA DI LEMONE Lemon Mousse, 69
TORTA AL MARSALA CON FRAGOLE Marsala Tart with Strawberries, 101
TORTA CIOCCOLATA CON NOCI Walnut Chocolate Tart, 46
TORTA DI FRUTTA FRESCA Fresh Fruit Tart, 45
ZABAGLIONE GATEAU, 152

FISH
BRANZINO AL BURRO FINNOCHIO Sea Bass with Fennel Butter, 116
CALAMARI RIPIENI CON FUNGHI Braised Squid Stuffed with Wild Mushrooms, 90
CAPPE SANTE AL BURRO CAMPARI Scallops with Campari Butter, 115
FETTUCCINE GIAN CARLO, 145
FILETTI DI SOGLIOLA PORTOFINO Filet of Sole Portofino, 39
GAMBERI NOCETO Shrimp with Nuts, 62
LUMANCHE SAN LORENZO Snails in Pasta, 140
PESCE ALLA VENEZIANA Venetian Fish, 93
RISOTTO AL CALAMARE Rice with Squid, 38
SALMONE AL FORNO Baked Salmon, 40
SALMONE CITRICO Salmon with Citrus Sauce, 62
SALMONE CON PORRI E ZAFFERANO Salmon with Leeks and Saffron, 89
SALMONE ROSSO IN LATTUGA RAPIENE Red Spring Salmon in Romaine Lettuce Stuffed with Mussels and Vegetable Julienne, 117
SCAMPI GIULIA, 143
TONNA ALLA SICILIANA Sautéed Tuna with Sicilian Vegetables, 92
TROTA IN CARPIONE Marinated Trout, 144

MEAT AND CHICKEN
ANIMELLE ALLA GRIGLIA CON
SALSA DI LIMONE E SALVIA
Grilled Sweetbreads with Lemon
and Sage Sauce, 119
ANIMELLE CON SCALOGNE
ARRISTE E SALSA DI MADEIRA
Sweetbreads with Roast Shallots
and Madeira Sauce, 94
BRODO DI VITELLO Veal Stock,
FILETTINI DUE PEPI Filets of Baby
Beef, 42
LOMBATA D'AGNELLO AL FORNO
Roast Loin of Lamb, 44
LOMBATO DI VITELLO RIPIENO
CON SALSA DI SALVIA Veal Loin
Stuffed with Wild Mushrooms with
Sage Sauce, 122
LONZA DI MAIALE ARROSTO CON
FICHI, CIPOLLE, PIGNOLE E
MARSALA Roast Pork Tenderloin
with Figs, Scallions, Pine Nuts and
Marsala, 96
MANZO AL FUNGHETTO Beef
Tenderloin with Mushrooms, 66
MANZO ALLA BOSCAIOLA Stuffed
Beef Tenderloin, 41
PETTO DI POLLO ALLA SALVIA
Chicken Breasts with Sage, 68
PICCATA DI POLLO AL LIMONE
Breast of Chicken in Lemon, 43
POLLO AI FERRI CON POMODORI
FRESCA Grilled Chicken with
Tomato Relish, 125
POLLO AL FORNO DELLA NONNA
Grandmother's Roast Chicken, 148
POLLO ALLA CARCIOFI E
ZINZERO Braised Chicken with
Artichokes and Ginger, 97
ROLE DI MANZO Pinwheel of Beef
Tenderloin with Spinach and
Smoked Salmon, 120
SCALLOPINE DI VITELLO
BOSCAIOLA Veal Scallopine, 67
SCALOPPINE DI VITELLO Veal
Scallopine with Fennel and Cream,
95
SCALOPPINI DI VITELLO CON FIN-
OCCHIO Veal with Fennel, 146

VITELLO ALLE PERE Veal with
Pears, 65

PASTA
CONCHIGLIE BUONE Noodles with
Prosciutto, 57
FARFALLINE ROMANTICHE
Butterfly Pasta with Prosciutto and
Asparagus, 88
FETTUCCINE "ARLECCHINO", 57
FETTUCCINE GIAN CARLO, 145
FETTUCCINE IOLANDA, 142
FETTUCCINE MODO MIO, 142
FUSILLI CON RAPINI, FUNGHI E
POMODORI Spiral Pasta with
Rapini, Wild Mushrooms and
Tomatoes, 86
FUSILLI MARINARA Seafood
Spirals, 61
LINGUINE ALLA SALSA DI
VONGOLE Linguine with Red
Clam Sauce, 33
LUMANCHE SAN LORENZO Snails
in Pasta, 140
MACCHERONCINI AL
GORGONZOLA Small Macaroni
with Gorgonzola, 59
MANICOTTI DELLA NONNA
Grandmother's Manicotti, 32
PENNE AL OCA AFFUMICATA
Pasta with Smoked Goose, 35
SCAMPI GIULIA, 143
SPAGHETTI AL AGLIO, OLIO E
PEPERONCINO Spaghetti with
Garlic, Oil and Hot Pepper, 60
TORTELLINI ALLA PANNA Stuffed
Pasta in Cream Sauce, 34

PIZZA
PIZETTA GIOVANNI, 86
PIZZETTA AL SARDINAIRA, 85
PIZZA DOUGH, 84

RISOTTO
RISOTTO NERO AL BALSAMICO,
140
RISOTTO AL CALAMARE Rice with
Squid, 38

SALADS
BINDI HOUSE DRESSING, 31
CACIOTTA DI CAPRA AL PEPE Goat
Cheese with Peppercorns, 113
CAROTE VINAIGRETTE Carrot
Vinaigrette, 112
INSALATA BINDI Bindi Salad, 30
INSALATA D'ENDIVA BELGA,
PROSCIUTTO E PARMIGIANO
Belgian Endive (Chicory) Salad
with Prosciutto and Parmesan, 80
INSALATA DELLA CASA House
Salad, 29
INSALATA DI CACIOTTA DI
CAPRA CALDO Warm Goat's
Cheese Salad, 112
INSALATA DI FARFALLE FREDDE
Cold Butterfly Pasta Salad, 55
INSALATA DI MANISCALCO
Blacksmith's Salad, 137
INSALATA DI POMODORI E
CIPOLLINI Tomato and Onion
Salad, 56
INSALATA DI RADICCHIO E
LATTUGA VERDE Mixed Salad, 55
INSALATA DI TONNO CON
FAGIOLE E POMODORO Fresh
Tuna, Bean and Tomato Salad, 79
INSALATA GENARO Tomato and
Arugula Salad with Roast Garlic
Dressing, 81
INSALATA RADICCHIO Radicchio
Salad, 30
INSALATA RUSSA Russian Salad,
137
SALSA PER INSALATA Oil and
Vinegar Dressing, 29
VINAIGRETTE, 114

SAUCES & DRESSINGS
Bechamel Sauce, 37, 149
BINDI HOUSE DRESSING, 31
BRODO DI VITELLO Veal Stock, 147
Buerre Manié, 36
Crème Fraîche, 45
PESTO Basil Paste, 151
RAGU DI FAGIOLI Bean Sauce, 150
SALSA BASILICA FRESCA Fresh
Basil Cream, 109

SALSA BESCIAMELLA Bechamel
Sauce, 37, 149
SALSA DI POMODORO ALL'ILVA
Ilva's Tomato Sauce, 149
SALSA DI POMODORO Tomato
Sauce, 64
SALSA DI SALVIA Sage Sauce, 124
SALSA MARINARA Tomato Sauce,
36
SALSA PER INSALATA Oil and
Vinegar Dressing, 29
SAN GIACOMO DRESSING (for
antipasto), 26
VINAIGRETTE, 114

SOUPS
BISQUE DI CIPOLLE Red Onion
Bisque, 110
MINESTRA DI GRANO Corn
Chowder, 110
MINESTRA PEPERONI FREDDO
Chilled Roast Pepper Soup, 82
MINESTRONE NOSTRANO Mixed
Vegetable Soup, 138
STRACCIATELLE Egg and Cheese
Broth, 138
ZUPPA D'AMARENA FREDDA Cold
Cherry Soup with Pernod, 27
ZUPPA DI PATATE Potato Soup, 139
ZUPPA DI PESCE CAPRESE Capri
Seafood Soup, 83
ZUPPA POMODORA AL
FINNOCCHIO Tomato and Fennel
Soup, 27

VEGETABLES & LEGUMES
RAGU DI FAGIOLI Bean Sauce, 150
ZUCCHINI AI FERRI Grilled
Zucchini, 126